the bible
with pleasure

the bible with pleasure

Stephen Motyer

Crossway Books

Leicester

CROSSWAY BOOKS
38 De Montfort Street, Leicester LE1 7GP, England
Email: ivp@uccf.org.uk
Website: www.ivpbooks.com

First published 1990 by Scripture Union
Revised edition 1997
Reprinted 2000, 2001

British Library Cataloguing in Publication Data
A catalogue record for this book is available from the British Library.

ISBN 1-85684-147-2

Set in Palatino

Typeset in Great Britain by Textype Typesetters, Cambridge

Printed in Great Britain by
The Guernsey Press Co. Ltd., Guernsey, Channel Islands

CONTENTS

Preface

I am an enthusiast for the Crossway Bible Guides. I think that, potentially, they are life-transforming for the groups (and individuals) who use them. So I regard it as a great privilege to be the New Testament editor for the series. Gradually we are refining the layout so that they become more and more user-friendly, revealing the fruits of in-depth study and guiding the practical application of God's Word to our lives.

I was really pleased when the opportunity arose to revise this little book, which I wrote some years ago, so that it could become a 'background' book for the series, setting out principles of interpretation for all the main types of literature in the Bible. It's not technical and I hope it's as readable as the Bible Guides themselves.

For those who want to know the differences between this book and its earlier version, *Unlock the Bible*, I should say that chapters 1–3 and 6 have largely been rewritten. The rest have just been tinkered with.

If this little book helps the Crossway Bible Guides to be more fruitful in their ministry, I shall be glad indeed – and that's my prayer.

Christmas 1996 *Stephen Motyer*

'I met someone who said . . .'

Mr Worthington stood at the door, friendly, polite. 'I've brought back your toaster, Mr Motyer. There wasn't much wrong with it.'

We were pleased to have 'found' Mr Worthington living only a few streets away – a retired electrician who still liked to keep his hand in with small repair jobs.

'Oh, thank you,' I replied. 'What was the trouble?'

Mr Worthington looked at the ground. 'Well, someone had obviously tried to mend it and not reassembled it properly; the thermostat was wrongly connected.'

I felt he knew well who the 'someone' was, but I hoped that my pink cheeks did not give me away as I thanked him and invited him in.

Yes, I was the guilty party. It's amazing how many small parts there are in an ordinary toaster. I had laid out all the little screws and nuts in the right order, or so I thought. But obviously I had got it wrong. The toaster worked for a while, but eventually my mistake showed up and we had to find an expert to put it right. Mr Worthington was not a groping amateur, like me. He had a lifetime's experience to guide him, as well as the relevant manuals. He is probably rather glad of people like me, because we certainly ensure a constant supply of work! We like to think that our common sense will see us through, and that the little knowledge we have picked up here and there will be enough.

If I had had the manual and the proper exploded diagram, I probably could have mended the toaster myself. But, failing that, Mr Worthington was the answer.

The same is true spiritually. We like to think we have enough understanding of our faith to cope with the challenges of everyday life, but, if we need extra help, most of us have a pastor, vicar or close Christian friend – the equivalent of Mr Worthington – to whom we can look for guidance. Such people can look up the manual of the spiritual life, the Bible, on our behalf, and interpret it for us. It's great to have them around.

But is it right to let the Bible recede to a distance from us like this? Even Christians who never read the Bible personally are still dependent on it for their understanding of what it means to be a Christian. They may actually be relying on the guidance of their pastor or church, and we can thank God for reliable guides to the way of Jesus – but how can we be sure that, somewhere down the line, the Bible has not been misinterpreted, so that everyone who relies on the teaching of our particular pastor, church or evangelist is actually being misled? 'I met someone who said . . .' could be an excuse for not thinking things out for ourselves.

Why bother with the manual?

There is actually no substitute for getting to grips with the manual ourselves. We *must* 'bother' with it – and there are three big rewards for doing so.

1. We shall get to know Jesus for ourselves

The whole Christian life is a challenge to listen to Jesus, to learn from him, and then to put into practice what we hear. The Christian life is a personal relationship with him. How can we possibly develop our relationship with him without listening to him? If we depend wholly on the spiritual equivalents of Mr

Worthington, how shall we ever really get to know Jesus Christ for ourselves?

Strangely, getting to know Jesus by going straight to the manual will also mean getting to know ourselves. One of the devil's most common and effective tactics is to make us blind to our true spiritual state before God. He managed this very successfully with the church in Laodicea (Rev. 3:14–22). They thought, 'I am rich . . . and do not need a thing', but Christ saw them as 'wretched, pitiful, poor, blind and naked' (verse 17). The word 'blind' is the key. They could not see themselves as they really were, and deluded themselves that they had arrived, spiritually. Many of us are living in that same spiritual state today.

In fact, the Laodiceans just needed to hear Jesus speak. A little letter came to them from John, passing on to them the words of the risen Christ about them. It was Jesus' direct word to them, and it tore aside the veil of their blindness and revealed to them what they really were. They looked into the mirror that Jesus held up to them and were horrified by what they saw. But along with that awful revelation came Jesus' loving appeal, 'Open the door, and I will come in!' (*cf.* verse 20), and his offer of the spiritual clothing and healing they so desperately needed (verse 18).

We need to hear Jesus speaking directly to us, in rebuke and encouragement, like this. The Laodiceans were given a special privilege. In all likelihood we shall not hear his voice directly until we stand before his judgment seat, and then it will be too late to discover how wrong our self-assessment has been. If we are to grow closer to him now we must hear him speak now – and he has done so in the Bible.

2. We shall develop a first-hand faith

A second-hand faith is always inadequate. Our teachers may be excellent and our church vibrant, but we still need to develop our own understanding of what Christianity is all about. Part of the trouble with the Corinthian church was that they were still

11

tied to their teachers' apron-strings. They were even boasting, 'My teacher's better than yours!' (*cf.* 1 Cor. 1:12). Because of this, Paul had to tell them to grow up. He calls them 'mere infants in Christ', not yet ready for 'solid food' (1 Cor. 3:1–2). They lacked a solid grounding in the faith. And so, when faced with teachers who were saying different but complementary things, they thought they must be in radical disagreement with each other and started taking sides:

'I follow Paul!'

'I follow Apollos!'

'I follow Cephas!'

'I follow Christ!'

They needed to learn to discriminate and to have a mature understanding of the faith, in which the differences between these teachers were put into proper perspective. This is what Paul tries to give them in 1 Corinthians 3 (and in the letter as a whole).

Paul makes this kind of mature judgment a goal to achieve, in Romans 12:1–2. How do we make decisions, as Christians? Are we just pushed from behind by our background and instincts? Or pulled from in front by our desires and expectations? Or are we able to exercise a 'renewed mind', and 'test and approve what the will of God is'? It's a big challenge – but we shall never even begin to do this without getting to grips with the manual.

3. We shall become equipped to follow Jesus

When eating abroad, the first step is to have the menu translated so that we can understand it. But this is not enough in itself. The vital thing is to choose a meal and eat it. Similarly, it is vital to know the way of Jesus, but even more vital to be equipped to follow it.

And this is where the Bible is different from the kind of manual I might have consulted about my toaster. It is not just a source of information about God: it is also a source of power, which really can change us if we will be open to it. In fact, the Bible is a wonderful means of personal growth. All down the centuries, Christian people have discovered its amazing power to change us for the better.

How does it do this? The quick answer is: because the Holy Spirit uses it. But we can unpack this a little. Jesus commands us to 'love the Lord your God with all your heart and with all your soul and with all your mind' (Mt. 22:37), and for Christians this is the supreme goal. If we can do that, then we shall fulfil our destiny as human beings. The three words 'heart', 'soul' and 'mind' refer to different aspects of our make-up, and in each case the Bible has a vital role to play.

- The heart is the seat of our *affections* – our emotions, desires, feelings. These are so often the things that lead us astray. Uniquely, by the beauty and truthfulness of its stories and its imagery, the Bible will gradually train us not to be attracted by worthless things, and to love what is right and wholesome, and the God who is supremely beautiful.
- The soul is the seat of our *volitions* – our will, decisions and determination. As we feed on the truths of the Bible, our determination to love the Lord and serve him will be strengthened.
- The mind is the seat of our *cognitions* – our thinking and understanding. In fact, we shall not be able to love God at all unless we understand something of his nature, and of his love for us. And only in the Bible do we hear that story.

Many Christians, I believe, have lost the vision of personal development. It is probably true that there is not much, if anything, that we can do about our personalities. These are a gift from God to us, the fruit of his creative decisions. My wife and I were very impressed with the way in which, even as babies, our children showed the special marks of person-ality which continue to distinguish them as they grow up. In our basic personality make-up, God does not want us to change. We need to accept ourselves as God has made us, as far as personality is concerned. We would be spared a lot of psychological trauma if we could accept and love ourselves as God does.

But our characters are a different matter. We need to work on these. We must strive for character-change, because we need to love God more, to serve his children better, to pray with more eagerness, to be less temptable, in fact to become more Christlike. Of course, different types of personality produce distinct traits of character, so it is impossible to distinguish in a hard-and-fast way between the two. A forceful, dominant person may have to work extra hard at 'listening skills' and at being sensitive to the unspoken needs of others, while this may come more naturally to more tolerant types. We are all very different, but we all need to have the character of Christ formed within us. And in this operation the Bible is one of the Surgeon's most essential instruments.

Tearing off the wrappings

There is security in the knowledge that, if the toaster breaks down, I can mend it. The only way that I could acquire that security would be to get the necessary manual, tear off the wrappings, and get down to study. Then I would not need to call for Mr Worthington. Similarly, there is great spiritual security in knowing where we stand before God.

Paul hits the nail on the head in 2 Corinthians 3:18. He considers the time when Moses had to veil his face because, after he spoke with God, it shone with dazzling brightness (Ex. 34:29–35). This veil was necessary because the Israelites could not face God themselves; they could not even bear his glory reflected in Moses' face. So Moses had to act as a go-between, bringing them God's word. But Paul comments that, like Moses, we have now been privileged to enter the very presence of God, in Christ: 'And we, who with unveiled faces all reflect the Lord's glory, are being transformed into his likeness with ever-increasing glory.' This is revolutionary! It turned upside down Paul's whole understanding of God's purposes. The humblest

Christian believer is in the same position as the mighty Moses himself!

But it is tragic that we are so eager to replace that veil, to put the wrappings back on and to retreat into the Old Testament situation where God's people had to depend wholly on Moses to bring God's word to them. We are so easily content to rest on the ministry of others and to let the veil of busyness, indifference or sin cloud our personal vision of the Lord. We laugh at those who think they are experts just because they 'met someone who said . . .', but we can be just like this in the spiritual sphere. If we want to get to know God better, many things will be important – prayer, fellowship, worship, practical service. But at the heart of it all is the Bible, for it will give us insight into the heart of God which we cannot obtain any other way. And as our vision is clarified, so our lives will be turned upside down.

'All Scripture is God-breathed and is useful for teaching, rebuking, correcting and training in righteousness, so that the man of God may be thoroughly equipped for every good work.' This is the dying Paul's prescription for Timothy's spiritual health, as he leaves the church in the young man's hands (2 Tim. 3:16–17). The prescription holds good today. Jesus' message to the Laodiceans was not just for them; the Spirit addressed their letter 'to the churches' (plural). And this is true, in God's plan, for the whole Bible. It was originally addressed to others, but the Spirit redirects it to us. As Paul wrote to the Romans, after packing his letter to them with quotations from the Old Testament: 'The whole Scripture was written to instruct us, so that we might have hope – through the endurance and the encouragement the Scriptures give us' (Rom. 15;4, my translation).

It is my prayer that this book, and the whole Crossway Bible Guides series, will enable the Scriptures to have that effect in many lives.

Doing what comes naturally

I would love to know what launched Mr Worthington into his career as an electrician. Maybe one day I shall know him well enough to ask. Perhaps his interest began when he sheltered from a shower of rain in an electricity showroom! But I am sure that he would never have made the grade in his chosen profession unless he had some aptitude for it. He had to learn the trade, of course, but his learning, I suspect, was grafted on to an instinctive ability which enabled him to make quick progress and to end up better at it than I would ever have been. My trouble is that I have little instinct for mechanical jobs, like repairing a toaster. I enjoy fiddling with things mechanical, but disaster often looms. The pincers in my tool-kit still bear the marks of the occasion when I used them to cut through a cable that was firmly plugged into the mains.

Friends of mine, although not formally trained as electricians, would have had no difficulty in repairing the toaster, because they are naturally mechanically minded. The Lord saw fit to make me different. Yet even I could do it, if I took a proper course of instruction. This raises an important question in the spiritual realm, because differences in aptitude and ability seem to appear there, too. In fact, the very presence of 'experts' in the church – the pastors, vicars, and leaders on whom we depend for teaching and guidance – can stifle the rest of us and make us feel that it is their job to 'handle' the Bible, not ours.

But the best ministers will tell you that, for all their training and experience, the Bible is there for everyone. There are no secret techniques revealed to them alone, no special formulae or private rules. Bible study is a public activity. So just as even I can have a go at mending my toaster, because I have a basic modicum of common sense – though it deserts me sometimes – so all Christians may feel that the Bible is their book; theirs to interpret and apply to life today.

The basic essentials

Astronomy, they say, is an amateur science. Anyone with a telescope can study the stars. The most famous British astronomer, Patrick Moore, has never received any formal training at all. And quite regularly, major discoveries have been made by amateur astronomers looking at the sky from their back gardens. The stars are simply *there*, and invite all to study them. In Bible study, too, the 'professionals' and the amateurs are really on the same level, standing amazed and fascinated before the sparkling variety and beauty of the Scriptures. What are the essentials that we all need, whether amateurs or professionals?

Patrick Moore will tell you the basic essentials for the astronomer: (1) enthusiasm, (2) the right equipment, (3) observational skills, and (4) experience and a trained instinct to be able to interpret and understand what you see. These four essentials all apply to Bible study, too!

1. Enthusiasm

My daughter is now just tall enough to qualify for most of the rides at the fun-fairs and theme parks we have visited recently. At the gate there is often a line to stand against: 'You must be as tall as this line to go on this ride.' Such disappointment, if she was a little short of the required height! But that's it: an absolute stop–start qualification. And enthusiasm is just like that, in the case of Bible study. If it's there, the doors are open wide. If it's not, there will be little learning and no excitement.

The editorial team for the Crossway Bible Guides, to which I am privileged to belong, is praying that the Guides will encourage enthusiasm for the Bible among the people and groups who use them. But this is actually a circular process: people need to be enthusiastic first, before they will get stuck into Bible study, perhaps with the help of one of the Guides. Then, we hope, their enthusiasm will grow.

We can encourage each other in this. It is much easier to generate enthusiasm in a group, and this is one of the reasons we have tried to make the Guides especially usable for group study. At rock bottom, we are talking about enthusiasm for Christ. Christians in love with him as their Lord will be keen to discover all they can about him and about following him.

2. The right equipment

Mr Worthington's home, I have no doubt, is full of all the vital bits and pieces he needs to repair the things people bring him. Patrick Moore has his own small observatory in his garden at Selsey in southern England. What equipment do we need in order to undertake effective Bible study – perhaps even to make discoveries?

It is like moving to, and settling into, a foreign country. I well remember the feeling of frustration and isolation my wife and I had, when we went to live in Germany with only a smattering of German at our disposal. If only we could communicate! As the weeks went by, we increased our knowledge and began to feel more at home, because we understood more.

Being a Bible student means overcoming a language barrier, also. The Bible was written in Hebrew, Aramaic, and Greek. If you took a degree course in biblical studies, you would probably find yourself learning at least one of these, and gaining much through acquiring this piece of equipment. But for most of us, the barrier has already been overcome, because the Bible is available in all the major languages of the world, and parts or all of it in many others, too. So we can read the Bible in our own language, and use our knowledge of our native tongue to understand it. This is a priceless privilege! We are prone to forget the tremendous sacrifices that were made so that we could have the Bible in our own lang·iage.

Of course, translations are always inadequate, especially translations of poetry, and of texts with lots of 'idioms'; that is, words and phrases with special meanings related closely to the culture and lifestyle of the native speakers. And that leads us to the second basic piece of equipment. Once my wife and I had learned some German, we could go on to the second stage of settling in – learning about German customs and lifestyle and getting to know our neighbours. This posed some problems. Innocently we went shopping one day, only to find everything boarded up. Apparently it was the day of an obscure religious festival, observed only in southern Germany. Similarly, we had to learn quickly what was expected of us when three small boys appeared at our flat after Christmas dressed as the three wise men, wanting to chalk a message on our door.

In both cases, our neighbours were a great help. They explained what we did not understand. It is the same with Bible study. We have to enter into the culture of the Bible, in order to understand it. And so we need the help of those who do. There is no short-cut! This book is full of examples of what this means. In later chapters we shall look in turn at different parts of the Bible, and time after time we shall see how vital it is to step into the shoes of the original writer or readers, so as to experience their world from within, and to understand it as if we were part of it ourselves.

We shall think more about this in the next chapter. For now, we just note how important it is to make this cultural adjustment. I live in a racially mixed area, with quite a number of Asian families in the streets around. Some of the older folk in these families, even after years in this country, still have very little English and so only a second-hand knowledge of the society and culture around them. I understand why this is, but I feel sorry for these folk. It seems like an opportunity missed, to cross barriers and enrich their lives (and ours). How much more a missed opportunity it is, when Christians prefer to remain dependent on their pastor or minister, and do not seek to become at home in the culture of Abraham, of Moses, of David, of Paul – or of our Lord Jesus himself.

There are many practical aids to help us feel at home in the Bible. The Crossway Bible Guides are just one of many available today. But that is their aim; for when we feel at home in the Bible, then we can begin to see for ourselves, like a group of people looking at the beauties of the moon or the planets for the first time through a powerful telescope.

3. Observational skills

Just having a telescope is no good. An astronomer needs to know how to focus and direct it, how to track stars across the sky, and how to record what he or she sees. We shall begin to think about the skills needed for Bible study in the next chapter, but in fact this whole book is about them. Bible study requires the development of some subtle skills. Like a beautiful work of art (which indeed it is), the Bible needs sensitive handling by skilled practitioners to draw out its meaning. And any one of us can do that!

4. Experience and instinct

These go together. The experienced astronomer will know at once if something unusual appears in his observations. And quite probably his instinct will immediately begin to suggest explanations for it. I well remember hearing Professor Anthony Hewish, who first observed pulsars, describing his discovery of these strange flashing objects in the sky. All his massive knowledge, experience and instinct were brought to bear as he tried to work out what these things could be. Gradually all the other explanations were eliminated, until eventually he and his team decided that they are enormously dense neutron stars, revolving very rapidly and sending out radiation in two beams, so that they appear to flash like a lighthouse.

Experience and instinct: these are vital for Bible study, too. Our experience of previous Bible study will be especially important, because as we read we are reminded of other passages and ideas which help us to understand. But in fact *every* sort of experience contributes to our reading of the Bible. Our family background, our conversion, the teaching and ethos of the church to which we belong, our varied experiences of life and of Christian service, and our understanding of the Christian gospel – all these form tools which we use to interpret the Bible. Obviously, this is usually helpful, but all these experiences are also like stained-glass windows through which the light of the biblical literature shines on to us. When we read it, it is coloured with all the hues of our own background and make-up – inevitably so.

This is an important point. As far as possible, we need to break free from interpreting the Bible simply on the strength of our own experience. We might well understand the Bible wrongly in some places because our background and experience may impart wrong 'colours' to it. For example, bad experiences of family life may make it hard for us to relate to God as 'Father'. We may be instinctively drawn to think of him as stern, forbidding and judgmental, and so to emphasize those elements in the biblical picture which seem to underline that. At the same time, we may be simply unable to absorb other aspects of the Bible's teaching about God the Father – his presence, approachability and self-sacrifice. Those 'colours' are blended out by the stained-glass window of our experience.

We need not despair. Once again, studying in a group is essential here. Because we are all different, we read Bible texts in subtly different ways. Of course, some contributions to a group discussion will just be wrong! But with good leadership, group Bible study will enable us to overcome the limitations of our own perspectives as we benefit from the different perspectives (and perhaps greater knowledge) of others.

And there is another type of 'instinct' which gives further hope that we shall be able to shake ourselves free from the controlling influence of our background and church experience. One of the most remarkable things about a conversion to Christ, and a living faith in him, is the way in which that experience brings the Bible to life. What was previously dead and uninteresting becomes meat and drink to the new believer. It is now full of meaning. When we become Christians a new 'instinct' is born – a spiritual awareness arising out of our new relationship with God. Now that we know the Author of the book, his words spring to life and make much more sense. It is the Holy Spirit, given to us when we become Christians, who makes the difference.

We can see this happening when the Holy Spirit was first given to the disciples. In his Pentecost sermon (Acts 2), Peter quoted three Old Testament texts, interpreting them all in dramatic new ways by applying them to the resurrection of Jesus and the events of that day. How was he able to do this so confidently? The reason appears a little later, in Acts 4:24–31. In prayer, the disciples remind God of what 'you spoke by the Holy Spirit through the mouth of your servant, our father David', and ask for boldness in the face of the persecution being threatened. God's response is immediate: 'They were all filled with the Holy Spirit and spoke the word of God boldly' (Acts 4:31).

So the Spirit who inspired David to write was acting again, this time enabling the church to speak 'the word of God'. In the same way, the Spirit enabled Peter on the day of Pentecost rightly to understand and interpret scriptures he had previously inspired. The Holy Spirit was indwelling the apostles, just as he had indwelt the prophets; so they had a kind of hotline to the Author. We can see evidence of this throughout the New Testament, as we note the way in which the authors quote and interpret the Old Testament.

Developing the right instincts

It is the same for us. We cannot hope to understand God's book unless the Holy Spirit tunes us in to his wavelength. But how does this actually work in practice? Should we expect to be inspired with understanding, as the apostles were? We need to tread carefully here. The answer seems to be, 'Yes – but not in the same way.' We can see the 'Yes' side in a remarkable passage in the first letter of John. John writes to the 'young men' of his church: 'you are strong, and the word of God lives in you, and you have overcome the evil one' (1 Jn. 2:14). So 'the anointing you received from him remains in you, and you do not need anyone to teach you' (2:27). If we have the 'anointing' of the Holy Spirit, so that God's word lives within us, then there is a sense in which we already have all we need. The apostles needed nothing more, and neither do we.

But John is writing from an ideal perspective. Life is not actually so simple, as Paul knew only too well. Though he thanked God for the gift of the Spirit to the Corinthians, he struggled to help them actually become 'spiritual' in their thinking and behaviour. (See, for example, 1 Cor. 1:4–7; 3:16; 3:1–4.) He makes the same point as John about the anointing of the Spirit when he writes: 'The spiritual man makes judgments about all things, but he himself is not subject to any man's judgment' (1 Cor. 2:15). But he knows, too, that it is possible to possess the Spirit and yet not to live spiritually. This is where Paul's apostolic ministry came in. He urged the Corinthians to follow his example (1 Cor. 11:1), which meant accepting his teaching as well as copying his lifestyle. Anyone who is truly spiritual and living in tune with God will, he said, 'acknowledge that what I am writing to you is the Lord's command' (1 Cor. 14:37). But Paul could not be so sure that the Corinthians would see it that way! They had much growing to do.

So this inbuilt 'instinct' for the Bible, given by the Holy Spirit himself, has to be developed in us. We simply do not become 'spiritual' overnight. It takes a lifetime, as we gradually grow into the right shape of mind and heart. As the great Baptist preacher C. H. Spurgeon put it, we need to pray and to study until 'our very blood becomes bibline'. In the process, God will use every experience he sends to us, and not just our study of his Word. Every new experience will shed new light on the Bible, and *vice versa*. In fact, our understanding of the Bible will grow in pace with the gradual transformation of our lives worked by the Spirit who inspired the Bible. As we become more and more like the Christ of whom the Bible speaks, so we shall more and more understand him – and it. Conversely, new insight into the meaning and teaching of the Bible will feed our growing knowledge and love of him.

Paul puts these two thoughts together in writing to Timothy. 'Do your best to present yourself to God as one approved, a workman who does not need to be ashamed and who correctly handles the word of truth' (2 Tim. 2:15). By 'correctly handling', Paul means literally 'cutting a straight path through'. Paul's thought is that Timothy must become trained to discern truth from error in the interpretation of the Bible and the gospel. In the midst of quarrelling and division (2:14, 16), Timothy is to seek to become the kind of person who knows his way confidently around 'the word of truth' – the gospel and the Scriptures that contain it.

That's a much better pattern on which to model our lives than 'I met someone who said . . .'!

Basic training

Even if Mr Worthington was the world's most gifted electrician, he could not dispense with the basic training necessary for his career. He probably served as an apprentice for several years, learning the job by watching a skilled electrician at work, and perhaps also attending night school. Only so could his instinct for that kind of work be refined and developed. As we saw in the last chapter, having an 'instinctive feel' for the job is important, but not enough. Though mechanically minded, Mr Worthington still needed to learn the right way to handle electricity and how to use the manuals and other tools of the trade.

The rules an electrician learns are set by the nature of electricity itself. Being what it is, it has to be handled in a certain way, and can be used only by particular machines. It is no use putting an electrical plug on the end of the hot-water inlet to the washing-machine. Nor can you warm up your bathwater by putting your electric fire into it! So it was vital that the training Mr Worthington received was right. Suppose he had actually been told to do what I discovered that you should never do to a live cable. The consequences would have been disastrous, both for him and for his future clients.

The same applies to Bible study. As Christians, we have an

'instinct' for understanding the Bible, because the Holy Spirit who inspired it lives in us. But we need to train ourselves in the right way of handling it. Otherwise, we may abuse it, without meaning to. And for us, too, the right principles of 'handling' are determined by the object being handled. A horse cannot be handled like a four-wheel-drive vehicle, even though both are forms of transport. A policeman cannot handle his dog as he would his riot shield, even though both are means of crowd control. And, similarly, there are methods of 'handling' that are suitable to the Bible, arising from its nature. If these are not employed, the Bible is as mishandled as a horse would be if its rider tried to run it on diesel.

What kind of training course?

In the last chapter we saw that we use ourselves to interpret the Bible. We cannot help filtering it through the net of our own experience, background and current understanding. This is absolutely inevitable – we can 'handle' it in no other way. So *we* have to change to match the Bible's teaching, and not *vice versa*, if we are going to handle it in a way that does not abuse it. God is in the business of changing us in just this way, using every experience of the Christian life to make us the kind of people who are able to 'cut a straight path through the word of truth' (2 Tim. 2:15, literally). We need to be, not stained-glass windows which impart alien colours to the light of God's Word, but prisms which reveal its true colours.

Unfortunately, it is easy to abuse the Bible by applying the wrong methods of interpretation to it. A horse would quickly make its discomfort clear if it was given diesel to drink. Similarly, it would be helpful if our Bibles closed themselves automatically whenever we misinterpret them! But sadly they do not. The Bible submits passively and silently to the most awful abuse. The effect of such mishandling is felt by us, who carry it out. And the consequences can be far-reaching. We can end up crowning some dreadful set of ideas with the authority of the Bible. It has happened over and over again in the history of the church, and happens still.

This means that we must reflect very carefully on the handling appropriate to the Bible and be constantly self-critical about what we think it teaches. If we have to change in order to understand it, then we must expect to grow in understanding, as in every other respect. We need to gain the knowledge appropriate to the handling of this particular animal.

Ground-rules

Three basic facts about the Bible should form the foundation of all Bible study. They are the ground-rules which the 'workman' must always observe. If we ignore these, we are sure to go wrong.

1. The Bible is history

It is easy to forget that the Bible is history, and we often ignore the implications of this. The Bible is a story – the story of God's dealings with his chosen people, and of his Plan to save the world. Within this overall history there are many individual stories. We meet prophets and kings, saints and sinners, heroes, crooks, simpletons, rebels and wise men, and we see how God dealt with them all. Above all, we meet Jesus and his individual history at the heart of the whole drama. Each person we meet, including every Bible author, was a real individual, living in a real situation. We see them either doing their best to live for God and to respond to his revelation of himself, or refusing to do so. Those who were responsive to God often found themselves involved in conflict and suffering, but constantly we see the power of God to bring his word to bear upon human need and to create joy in suffering and life out of death.

God used ordinary people to speak his word to others. Maybe the Bible authors were sometimes conscious of writing 'inspired Scripture', but generally they were just doing their best to fulfil the ministry that God had given them, in their particular time and place. Paul for instance, did not address his letters to the whole church, but to the particular congregations or individuals about whom he was worried. His aims in writing were no more ambitious than (for instance) to change the Galatians' mind about circumcision, or to sort out the Corinthians' extraordinary views on sex, or to help the Thessalonians get themselves straight on the second coming. Of course, God intended that these writings should form 'the Bible', the book to which all Christians look for instruction. But originally they were 'ordinary' pieces of human communication, produced by authors who wanted to minister to the special needs of particular groups of people.

It can come as a surprise to realize that the Bible was not written to us! We are just eavesdroppers. When we read the Bible, we are forming the third corner of a triangle, listening in to a conversation taking place between the other two corners. At one corner sits the human author of the passage we are reading. The first recipients or hearers of the word sit in the second corner. Between them, the author and the first recipients form the context of the word that God spoke. As we sit apart from both at the third corner, we 'hear' the message through the filter of our own concerns, which are probably very different from those of the author and first hearers. If we are to be true to the Bible, we must seek to distance ourselves from our own concerns, as far as possible. For the vital thing is what God said then. So we need to run a complete action replay of the original context, the situation of both author and readers.

Actually we can hear only one end of the conversation. Suppose you overhear someone on the telephone saying, 'You mean, you broke up yesterday afternoon?' The person at the other end of the line could have just ended a love affair, finished the school term or had an emotional collapse. The two people engaged in conversation know which of these is right, because the remark has a *context*, of which they are both aware. And until you are aware of it too, the remark will remain obscure. You could jump to a conclusion about it, but you would probably get it wrong.

In order to avoid jumping to false conclusions about the Bible, we need to know the whole story, if we can – to listen to both ends of the conversation. When we have done this action replay, and discovered what the problems were and what God said about them, then and only then shall we be ready to come back to the present and ask what God is saying to us today, through the same message.

This may sound as if the Bible is being taken away from us. How can it be our book, if it belongs to another time and place? The truth is, it can properly be ours only when we have allowed it fully to be theirs. We cannot gatecrash the conversation between the authors of the Bible and their first readers – compelling the Bible to mean something quite foreign to its original intention – any more than we can interrupt a telephone conversation and tell the participants what they really meant to say. If the Bible has an inspired meaning, then that meaning must be basically what it meant when first communicated.

2. The Bible is literature

When we describe the Bible as 'literature', this is not as intimidating as it might sound. God has chosen to give us a book which is a product of language, like any other book. This really follows from the first point, that the Bible is history: just as the author and first readers made up a real-life situation in which God spoke to them, so the communication of God's word to them made use of real-life language and communication skills.

For many years, scholars believed that the Greek of the New Testament was a special language, used only by the Holy Spirit in the production of inspired Scripture. It seemed to be unique when compared to the literary products of contemporary Greek writers. But at the beginning of this century, archaeologists unearthed other kinds of writing from the first century AD, particularly from several sites in Egypt, where some very 'ordinary' kinds of communication had been preserved – scraps of correspondence, notes, shopping-lists. And they discovered that these were written in Greek very similar to that of the New Testament! So it turned out that, far from using a special language, the New Testament was written in the language of the common people, which was spurned by the literary artists of the day. This should have been expected, really. Paul says that he deliberately did not use 'wise and persuasive words' (1 Cor. 2:4), that is, the kind of high-flown language with which travelling philosophers baffled their hearers. And, in their turn, his opponents (who modelled themselves on these philosophers) said scathingly of Paul that 'his speaking amounts to nothing' (2 Cor. 10:10).

Paul, like the other Bible authors, used the language of the people because he really wanted to communicate. He wrote in a direct, unpolished way, sometimes even in slang. This creates difficulties for us 2,000 years later, for nobody today speaks the language of the New Testament. There are a large number of Greek writings surviving from the period immediately before the New Testament, but these all use the 'classical' Greek language and style, the polished language of education and public affairs. We need to go beyond these and tune in to the grass-roots language in which most of the New Testament is written. Only so shall we be able to listen in to the conversation between the other two corners of the triangle.

The Old Testament faces us with the same problem even more acutely. There are no other surviving examples of ancient Hebrew literature at all. So scholars have particular difficulties with words that occur only once or twice in the Old Testament. What do they mean? Normally, the meaning of words is discovered first by looking at the meaning of related words, and secondly, by observing the contexts in which they are used. Thinking back to the overheard telephone conversation, you would immediately know the meaning of 'broke up' if the next thing you heard was: 'You must be pleased, with the holidays to look forward to.' This kind of remark fits only one of the three possible meanings of 'break up'. In the same way, scholars use context to determine the meaning of biblical words.

But more than one context is necessary to gain a rounded definition of a word. And even if a word appears frequently in the Old Testament, its appearances may be scattered over more than 1,000 years. There was plenty of opportunity for the meaning of words to change between Moses and Malachi! We need only reflect, for instance, on the change in the meaning of the English word 'nice' over the last 400 years: it used to mean something bad ('silly', 'fussy'), and then 'precise'. It actually started life as the Latin word *nescius*, 'ignorant'. But now it has lost its bad flavour altogether.

The answer to these difficulties is simply to be as vigilant as possible about the context – and surprisingly this is where the ordinary reader, as opposed to the scholar, comes in. Scholars, with all the technical expertise at their disposal, can tell us what the likely meanings of rare words are, and can show us how the meanings of words changed with the passage of time. But in the long run, what matters is the actual use of words to form sentences and paragraphs that really communicate. The author of the book of Revelation, for instance, used many words in a new way and broke all the rules of Greek grammar, in trying to get across to his readers the other-worldly realities he had seen. Scholars can analyse the extraordinary Greek he uses. But in wrestling with the actual meaning of the words in context, the Greek expert has no great advantage over the ordinary reader.

This is because interpretation is a delicate human science. We sympathize with the author and his readers, sensing the meaning of the text. We need to equip ourselves with as much knowledge as we can, but the vital thing is that sense of the real, living communication going on along the opposite side of the triangle.

A picture of this conversation is built up as we keep asking 'Why'? about the text in front of us. Something impelled the human author of Scripture to say *this* first, and to follow it with *this*, before going on to *that*. Why? As we discover the connection of thought that led him, and relate it to all we know about the readers and their situation, two things will happen.

First, we shall be able to see how individual words and phrases are given more precise and delicate shades of meaning by the paragraphs in which they are used. The surrounding context shapes the meaning of each of the words, phrases and sentences within it.

Secondly, we shall gain a sense of the whole message, built up from the study of its parts. We shall be better able to say, 'What God wanted to say to the Philippians was . . .' and be more sure that we are getting to the heart of the matter.

3. The Bible is a library

The idea that the Bible is a library follows on from the previous two points. It contains many different kinds of book: gospels, letters, prophecies, psalms, and so on. Awareness of all these different types is a vital ingredient in the right handling of the Bible. When we talk to others, we instinctively classify what we hear or say into different types of utterance. We know the difference between a joke and a confession, between a sermon and a lullaby. Great confusion (and offence) would result if we started to muddle these up! Each type of utterance has its appropriate kind of response.

But what is instinctive for us in everyday life has to be painstakingly learned in Bible study. As we listen in to the conversation taking place along the opposite side of the triangle, we need to be able to identify and rightly interpret the types of utterance which the biblical authors and their readers used instinctively.

It is easy to blur the distinctions between the various books in this 'library'. As we wander around its shelves we meet, for instance, *gospels*. A 'gospel' is a particular type of literary product – and, in fact, a type unique to the Bible. Recently, quite a lot of scholarly discussion has gone on over the question, 'Are the gospels a unique type of literature?' There seem to be some fairly close parallels, but it is clear that Matthew, Mark, Luke and John did not slavishly follow a set literary pattern. They moulded the conventional pattern to match their unique purpose. And so a unique type of literature was invented in connection with Jesus of Nazareth!

How did they come to be called 'gospels'? The reason is not hard to find. Originally, 'gospel' meant 'the preaching of the good news'. When Paul declared, 'I am not ashamed of the gospel' (Rom. 1:16), he meant that he was not ashamed of his ministry as an apostle, commissioned by God to tell the good news of Jesus to all and sundry.

It was Mark who began the change in meaning whereby the word 'gospel' came to be applied to the first four books of the New Testament. He starts his book with the words, 'The beginning of the gospel about Jesus Christ, the Son of God' (Mk. 1:1). He felt that the good news of Jesus had a 'beginning'. Like Paul, he too wanted to minister that good news to others, probably to the persecuted Christians of Rome. He felt that the best way to do this was to take them back to the 'beginning' and tell them the story of Jesus, starting with John the Baptist and relating especially how Jesus faced persecution and martyrdom and called his disciples to follow in his footsteps. So the gospel form arose out of the ministry of the gospel message, in a particular setting. The other gospel-writers followed suit, because for them too the form suited the purpose for which they wrote.

We may say the same about all the different types of literature in the Bible library. In each case, the form matches the purpose and is part of the communication along that opposite side of the triangle. The gospels are a special example of Bible *history*, and all the history books of the Bible have a special concern. They were intended not simply to inform about the past, but also to encourage and instruct the readers about how they should live in the present.

Alongside history there is a large category which we can label *prophecy*. We attach this label to the writings of 'the prophets', who were commissioned to speak in God's name to his people, apparently ministering to their needs more directly than the authors of biblical history. There are New Testament prophets to match the Old Testament ones: Paul and the apostles thought of themselves as prophets in the Old Testament sense, and their preaching style probably matched that of the Old Testament prophets. But when Paul ministered through writing, he did not send transcripts of his sermons but wrote *letters*, thus employing another literary form, adapted to his own purposes.

There is another broad class of Bible literature, related to prophecy, called *apocalyptic*. We find this kind of writing particularly in the book of Revelation in the New Testament, and in Daniel and Ezekiel in the Old. It involves visions and vivid imagery, sometimes clearly intended to predict the future, and it requires great sensitivity in interpretation. It is possible to go gravely wrong here, probably more so than with any of the other types of biblical writing. And the error usually arises precisely from failing to recognize that apocalyptic is a style or form of writing deliberately adopted for a particular purpose, so that special rules of interpretation apply. These rules need to be discovered and carefully observed, or the horse will be fed on diesel.

Then there are biblical prayers, or *psalms*. These too are a literary form, deliberately used as a medium of communication for a particular purpose. As we shall see, the psalms were not just private prayers, but had a public function as well: they were ways of speaking to other people as well as to God, very much like our hymns today. Closely linked to the psalms is another kind of writing, often called *wisdom literature*. Some of the psalms are themselves examples of this type, but the books of Job, Proverbs, Ecclesiastes and (in the New Testament) James are the fullest representatives of it in the Bible.

Prophetic, apocalyptic and wisdom literature overlap considerably in places. Jesus himself makes use of all three styles in his own teaching, and this must affect the way we interpret it. The 'wisdom' background is especially clear in passages like the Sermon on the Mount (Mt. 5 – 7), and Mark 13 is a piece of pure apocalyptic. Jesus' direct denunciation of the scribes and Pharisees in Matthew 23 has a very 'prophetic' flavour. Paul uses apocalyptic language in some of his letters, for instance in 1 Thessalonians 4:13 – 5:11; and clearly draws on wisdom models in writing some of his practical instructions, for instance in Romans 12.

In addition to these broad, interlocking categories, there are smaller literary styles or forms, each of which must also be treated carefully and interpreted according to its own rules. One of the most important of these is the *parable*, of great significance in Jesus' teaching. Another is the *literary speech*, which Luke uses frequently in the book of Acts. Luke's first readers would have known what significance to attach to the speeches in Acts, because of their awareness of the use of this particular literary device by other authors. Then there are the *household code* (see (Eph. 5:22 – 6:9); the *virtue and vice catalogue* (see Rom. 1:29–32); the *genealogy* (see Mt. 1:1–17); the *macarism* (a saying which begins 'Blessed is . . .'; see Ps. 1; Mt. 5:3–12); the *hymn* (snatches of songs from the worship of the early church are quoted in 1 Tim. 3:16 and Eph. 5:14); the *diatribe* (a particular style of preaching, also known outside the New Testament; see Rom. 8:31–39); and a host of other technical labels, which can be attached to different forms of speech or literary types. All of them need to be identified and carefully handled.

That is what this book is all about. In the chapters that follow, we look in turn at each of these larger types of literature, asking in each case how this particular animal should be handled. (We shall touch on some of the smaller types as we go.) Each of these chapters forms an introduction to the study of a section of the Bible. If you are using a Crossway Bible Guide to a book that falls into one of these types, then you will find it helpful to read the relevant chapter in this book as introduction and back-ground. All the way through, we shall build on these three basic facts about the Bible: it is history, it is literature and it is a library. These facts are the compass-bearings on which we set our course.

So off we go!

'Just want the fax, ma'am!'

Learning from Bible histories

'Just want the fax, ma'am' is a family saying in our home. It dates from a rather ancient American crime series in which this was a favourite remark of one of those hard-bitten TV cops. Sergeant Webb, I think he was called. Faced with a weeping, raging or otherwise emotional female, this cop would cut through the fog of feeling with a gruff reminder that he, at least, was not going to be carried away, but just wanted 'the fax'.

The truth about 'the fax'

Can you separate facts from feelings? Or – to put it differently – is it possible just to describe something, without also expressing an opinion about it? At first sight the answer seems a clear 'Yes'. The football commentator could just describe what he sees without adding remarks about the quality of the play (good or bad). A policeman could just describe 'the fax', without making any judgment about whether a crime had been committed or not. But in fact, if they did this, we would probably feel that they were not doing their jobs properly. They are trained to interpret what they describe.

And in any case, interpretation often happens without being noticed. Even if he has been told, for some reason, not to assess the play, the commentator will still describe what happens on the ball. He will not concentrate on the referee's chic new outfit, or tell us in detail how the goalkeeper ties his shoelaces. Similarly, even though he may not express an opinion about it, the policeman will describe the events which might be criminal and will ignore the fact that a flock of pigeons was flying overhead at the time. In doing this, both are already interpreting what they see. The interpretation is implicit in their choice of what to describe, but it is no less real for that.

In fact, we should state two important rules about history in general, before we look at histories in the Bible.

1. All history is interpretation

It is a rather disturbing thought, but it is true: as soon as something is past, it is accessible only through the filter of our capacity to interpret and understand. Actually, this is true of the present, as well. We would live in a dim, twilight world if we were not constantly interpreting what was going on around us. The only difference in the case of the past is that the 'fax' come to us through our memories (or through someone else's), rather than through our eyes and ears. But they still need to be interpreted before they make any sense.

So any attempt to write up the past cannot just be a list of happenings; it would be completely useless if it were. As soon as the list is less than complete (that is, as soon as it leaves out something – anything – that occurred in the relevant period), an act of interpretation has taken place. We would then want to ask the author of the list why he rated this or that happening as less important than the things he included. Since interpretation is inevitable, it is better if a historian does not keep quiet about his reasons, but makes his principles of interpretation clear. We can then decide whether he is right or not.

2. All history-writing is prompted by the present

When historians write, they are prompted to do so by present concerns or pressures. They would not write if they did not feel that they could meet present needs by doing so. It may only be a desire to understand the present by comparing it with the past, or to keep the past alive for future generations. More grandly, they may want to help their contemporaries not to repeat the mistakes of the past. There may be many different motives. But some such motive will always be present.

These two general comments are very important for understanding the history books which form a large segment of the Bible. In this chapter, we shall concentrate on the Old Testament, where everything up to and including the book of Esther may be classified as 'history' – seventeen books in all. We shall look at the New Testament histories (the gospels and Acts) in chapter 6.

Although we classify these books as 'histories', the Bible does not call them this. In fact, most of the books concerned were classified in New Testament times under the heading 'Torah', which means 'law' or 'instruction'. This shows that the biblical authors and readers were well aware of the two points we made above. They consciously wrote from a particular viewpoint, interpreting the past in the light of their understanding of God and his Plan, and wanting to 'instruct' and encourage God's people in their present life of faith and obedience. This is why these books of history include within them what we usually call 'the law' (the instructions given through Moses about the life-style demanded of God's people, in Exodus, Leviticus, Numbers and Deuteronomy), just as the gospels include passages like the Sermon on the Mount (Mt. 5 – 7).

None of these Bible histories sets out to be a full, blow-by-blow, detailed chronicle. In fact, all of them are highly selective, recording only the events which (a) illustrate their understanding of the meaning of the history they are writing up, and so (b) communicate the message they want to convey. Modern historians accuse them of being biased because they do this. But all historians do it, not just religious ones. We cannot blame the Bible historians for writing with a purpose which does not match the interests of historians today. For instance, we know from sources outside the Bible that Jeroboam II (793–753 BC) was possibly Israel's most powerful king, extending his influence further even than King David had done. Modern historians, interested in the politics and economics of the time, would like to know more about him – but the Bible passes over his prosperous forty-year reign in almost total silence (2 Ki. 14:23–29), mentioning the expansion but summarizing his reign with the words, 'He did evil in the eyes of the LORD and did not turn away from any of the sins of Jeroboam the son of Nebat, which he had caused Israel to commit' (verse 24). For the writer, that was all that mattered.

Similarly, the gospels pass in almost total silence over the first thirty years of Jesus' life, and 'the Acts of the Apostles' boil down to 'the Acts of Peter and Paul'. Modern historians regret such 'imbalance'. They would write a history of Jesus with different concerns and interests. But maybe they would write with the *wrong* concerns and interests, so far as introducing their readers to the truth about Jesus is concerned. Their efforts would be no less acts of interpretation than those of our four evangelists. Yes, biblical histories are highly selective, but this does not disqualify them from being true.

Pointers to the message

In fact, being selective is absolutely vital for Bible history. For it claims to present a history of the world. One or two attempts have been made to write comprehensive world histories, but they are vast in comparison with the Bible. Yet this is the Bible's claim. (It actually has a broader scope than any other history, for it begins with creation in Gn. 1 and ends with the new creation in Rev. 21 – 22!) How can we discover the purpose of the historians who wrote these books and spot the message that they seek to get across to us? Here are some pointers.

1. Read the histories as a whole

The trouble with many Bible-reading schemes is that they

encourage a 'bitty' approach to reading. They give a shortish passage to read each day, and so make it hard for the reader to gain an overview of a whole book, or even of several books. To some extent this is inevitable, just because of the constraints of everyday life. Even the Crossway Bible Guides follow this kind of approach. But only certain parts of the Bible can legitimately be read in this way: that is, there are only a few books (Psalms, Proverbs, and possibly Jeremiah) where there is no overall design and plan for the book as a whole. Generally, the meaning of each part depends on its relation to the overall drama in which it is set, so we cannot afford to ignore the broad view.

It is therefore vital to try to get a sense of the broad sweep of the story, as well as an understanding of each incident within it. The Crossway Bible Guides try to provide this with introductory and survey sections at appropriate places, but it is quite difficult to achieve.

As a young Christian I attended a Bible study where we looked at the story of David and Mephibosheth in 2 Samuel 9:1–13. We gleefully turned the story into a picture of Christian conversion: Mephibosheth was handicapped (verse 3), picturing our sinful state before God. He lived in Lo Debar (verse 4), which means 'nothingness', reminding us of what life without Christ is like. David showed him God's kindness (verse 3), just as God has showered his grace on us. He showed this kindness for Jonathan's sake (verse 1), just as God saves us for Jesus' sake. And best of all, David brought Mephibosheth to sit at his table (verse 10), picturing our close fellowship and communion with God as Christians.

We ignored the bits that do not fit this technique, such as the fact that Mephibosheth was just as lame at the king's table as he had been before. It would not do to conclude that Jesus does nothing to remove our sin! But the biggest problem with this 'allegorizing' approach is that it does not take the story seriously as part of the whole history in which it sits. Mephibosheth was the grandson of Saul, the previous king. The normal procedure at this time, when one king displaced another, was for the entire family of the defeated dynasty to be wiped out. We see this happening to the family of Ahab in 2 Kings 10:1–11, when Jehu seized the throne. David does it to the rest of Saul's family – all but Mephibosheth – in 2 Samuel 21:1–9. He is hardly a picture of an all-forgiving God! In sparing Mephibosheth, he was keeping his promise to Jonathan (1 Sa. 20:14–17), but having him in Jerusalem under daily surveillance was undoubtedly a good way of keeping tabs on a potential rebel. Later, David was quick to judge Mephibosheth guilty of treachery (2 Sa. 16:3–4). So our allegorizing approach really did violence to the passage when we think of its wider context. We were miles from discovering its real meaning. And if we are going to learn the message of such a story for today, we must start with it as it is.

We may take a larger example from Genesis 12. The story of how Abram left Ur in obedience to God's call features high on the list of Sunday school favourites. What a sacrificial act of faith and trust! And of course it was. But Abraham's faith is not the main point of the story. World history turns a corner in Genesis 12. We come into this chapter from the tower of Babel in Genesis 11:1–9, where the story of how God's world has gone astray reaches a climax. The beautiful order and harmony of God's creation, underlined so strongly in the story at the start, have been ruined, until finally humankind is confused in language and scattered across the earth. Is that the end of the story, or does God have a Rescue Plan? Suddenly the zoom lens focuses on one individual, to whom God gives a command and a promise:

Leave your country, your people and your father's household and go to the land I will show you.

> I will make you into a great nation
> and I will bless you;
> I will make your name great,
> and you will be a blessing.

> I will bless those who bless you,
>   and whoever curses you I will curse;
> and all people on earth
>   will be blessed through you.

(Gn. 12:1–3)

Abram, and the nation descended from him, are to be God's means of rescuing the whole world. The whole drama of biblical history begins to unfold from this point. Even when it looks as though God is concerned only with Israel, we need to remember that his election of Abram and Israel has a wider purpose in view: he plans to save the world through them, and to re-gather scattered humanity through one nation which will be a 'blessing' to the rest. It is fascinating to reflect that, viewed from the perspective of Genesis 11, Abram's journey from Ur was just another example of the scattering inflicted upon humanity. But in Genesis 12 God begins to turn defeat into victory, by making this particular journey the first step towards the reunion of humankind.

The Old Testament books themselves encourage us to have this big overview, by looking backwards and forwards across the story they tell. For instance, in Deuteronomy 1 – 4 Moses reviews the whole history of Israel to date, and then in Deuteronomy 20 – 30 he looks ahead into the future and predicts what will happen after his death. Similarly, in 2 Kings 17 the writer looks back sadly over Israel's history of rebellion and disobedience in order to explain why God had banished her from the promised land – and we are able to say, 'How right Moses' predictions were!' We need to take the point and learn to develop this kind of approach, even though the circumstances of life compel us to tackle the Bible in small portions.

2. Watch for recurring themes and ideas

Thoughts which frequently surface are likely to be particularly important for the writer. For example, in the last section of the book of Judges, after the story of Samson which occupies the central chapters (13–16), we meet a little remark four times, once in the very last verse of the book: 'In those days Israel had no king; everyone did as he saw fit' (Jdg. 17:6; 18:1; 19:1; 21:25).

This little, repeated comment is sufficient to give the whole of Judges a particular flavour. The name of the book gives its theme: it records the ministry of the 'judges', who were God's means of rescuing Israel from various enemies. But the writer was clearly a monarchist, believing that the judges were not adequate to the task. Armed with this thought, we then reflect on the story of Samson in a new way and realize how inadequate he was, and how he squandered his resources and in fact led the people away from God. His story leads into two of the most depressing episodes in the whole Bible, as the last chapters of Judges (17 – 21) portray social disintegration and moral insensitivity to an extreme. The stories are told without comment on the rightness or wrongness of the behaviour described. We, the readers, are meant to make that judgment ourselves. All the writer gives us by way of interpretation is that suggestive little comment inserted into the narrative. Why did this happen? All because there was no king!

Another, bigger, recurring theme is that of covenant, or promise, which runs through all these histories. God's promise to Abraham in Genesis 12:1–3 is only the first of a long string of promises which follow on from each other as God moves his Plan onwards. The promise of universal blessing is frequently repeated and underlined by the direct intervention of God, even to the extent of enabling Abraham and Sarah to have Isaac in their old age. The promise of blessing for the rest of the earth begins to be fulfilled as Egypt is drawn into the story and is delivered from famine by Joseph. The last chapters of Genesis are full of promises, looking ahead into the future (see especially Gn. 49). God will bless and prosper the children of Jacob!

The theme of promise and covenant carries on through the drama of the exodus. When it seemed as though God had abandoned Israel, he 'remembered his covenant with Abraham, with Isaac and with Jacob' (Ex. 2:24) and stepped in to reaffirm his promise through Moses (Ex. 3:16–17). Later on, there is a further big renewal of the promise in connection with the appointment of the king in Jerusalem (2 Sa. 7:1–16). It is a fruitful and exciting theme to trace through these books.

Another such theme is that of the place, or the land. These histories present us with a succession of special 'places' chosen by God to be locations of encounter with him.

He promises Abraham the land of Canaan (Gn. 17:8), but the point of this gift becomes clear when God renews the promise to Jacob in Genesis 28:13–15. In a dream, Jacob sees heaven opened and hears the promise, 'I will give you and your descendants the land on which you are lying' (verse 13), and concludes, 'Surely the LORD is in this place . . . This is none other than the house of God; this is the gate of heaven' (Gn. 28:16–17).

It is at this point that we realize that the promised land is meant to be the place where God's people meet him. We think back to the garden of Eden and realize that this communion between humanity and God was what had been lost then. God seeks to re-establish it by setting apart a place where it may happen. We then understand how important, in the books which follow, is this idea of the place of communion with God. Moses' encounter with God at the burning bush starts off the exodus. That event reaches a climax at Mount Sinai, where God tells the people, 'I carried you on eagles' wings and brought you to myself' (Ex. 19:4), and where he reveals himself in thunder and smoke on the mountain. The book of Exodus ends with God's glory descending on to the tabernacle, called 'the tent of meeting', because it is there that God and humanity meet (Ex. 40:34–35). Eventually the temple is built in Jerusalem, designed to be just such a 'place'.

These lines of thought carry on even into the New Testament, where we discover that there is no longer a physical place, but a person, in whom God and humanity meet. His body is the temple (Jn. 2:19–21), and we become God's temple ourselves as we are built into Christ (1 Cor. 3:16–17; Eph. 2:19–22).

47

3. Look for the lesson

All the biblical stories have a 'point'; they are told for a reason. Sometimes the reason is clearly given within the stories themselves. But that is not always the case. For example, the story of how Solomon built the temple in Jerusalem is told with loving attention to detail, climaxing in the marvellous prayer of dedication in 1 Kings 8. The whole picture is so positive and grand that we might fail to notice the description of the gangs of forced labourers by whom the materials for the temple were quarried and transported (1 Ki. 5:13–18). But then we realize that Samuel's warning has been fulfilled. He told the people that the king they demanded would oppress them in this way (1 Sa. 8:11–18). There is a blot on the magnificence of the temple.

Samuel warned them too that 'When that day comes, you will cry out for relief from the king you have chosen, and the LORD will not answer you in that day' (1 Sa. 8:18). And so we are prepared for the further episode in 1 Kings 12, when the people petition Rehoboam, Solomon's son, to lighten 'the harsh labour and the heavy yoke' (1 Ki. 12:4) which his father had imposed on them – only to have the request sharply rejected.

These stories are subtly written. We need to be able to link separated passages in order to see the lesson the writer has in mind. One of the most striking episodes is the story of David's sin with Bathsheba, told in 2 Samuel 11 – 12. It is remarkable to see how uncompromisingly this dreadful account of lust, deceit, betrayal and murder is told, even about the mighty King David. Clearly, one of the lessons which the writer wants us to learn (though he never says so explicitly) is that violence breeds violence. David's seizure of Bathsheba and murder of her husband are replayed within his own family as we go on to hear of Amnon's rape of Tamar (2 Sa. 13:1–22), and then of Absalom's murder of Amnon for the deed (13:23–29). Pointedly, David takes no action against Amnon for doing something so similar to what he himself had done, even though we read that he was 'furious' when he heard (13:21). Similarly, he quickly forgives Absalom for his murder (13:39).

4. Be interested in individuals

This follows on from the last point. Throughout these histories there is a great emphasis on the place of individuals within God's Plan. The tone is set in Genesis 1 – 11, where no fewer than eighty-nine people are mentioned by name. Certain individuals play a major role in his Plan (Abraham, Moses, Joshua, Samuel, David), and we see what a premium he puts on working with and through human beings. This arises from that underlying emphasis on communion with him – the heart and goal of his whole rescue Plan.

This is what gives these stories their distinctive flavour. We meet real people here, very finely portrayed. We never get formal descriptions of character ('Now Samson had been spoilt as a much-longed-for, only child, and was never able to control his overdeveloped sex-drive' . . . 'Now Elijah had a "manic" temperament, inclined to alternate between heights of elation and depths of depression'), but it is not difficult to write such descriptions now. This sensitivity to the complexities of human character, combined with a mastery of the art of storytelling, puts some of the biblical stories at the head of the league of world literature. This is the right approach, I believe, to stories like that of David and Mephibosheth. The message of such stories appears as we study the characters involved, ask about their motives, and assess what they do in the light of God's dealing with them.

Some stand out. The story of Joseph is told with clarity and simplicity, but also with deep and subtle insight into human nature (Gn. 37 – 50). So too is the story of the rebellion of Absalom (2 Sa. 15 – 19). A host of minor characters people these books as well, and they all come across vividly and convincingly. We watch them following the Lord in faith, falling into disobedience and suffering the consequences, persevering through dreadful odds, being used by God in spite of their

49

failings, finding wisdom and courage beyond themselves, and falling victim to their own personality weaknesses – or overcoming them. And so they are a tremendous encouragement and education to us, as we see that God is vitally concerned with us as people, and can use anybody – even us – to take his Plan forward.

5. Observe the Plan

The overall plot, which holds all these books together and makes them one story, is God's Plan to save the world. This is actually the plot of the whole Bible, not just of the histories. It is this which, above all, links the histories to the prophets and unites the New Testament with the Old. From Abraham onwards, God's Plan focuses on Israel, with whom he has made a 'covenant', a promise to save. His relationship with Israel has constant ups and downs. Though he promises to be God to Abraham and to his descendants for ever (Gn. 17:7), and though he promises to maintain King David's family on the throne of Israel for ever (2 Sa. 7:16; 1 Ki. 9:5), things get so bad that eventually Israel loses the promised land and the line of kings is broken.

This is merely the last and most dreadful of many crises in the working of the covenant. And yet through them all we are able to see God's patient determination to persevere with Israel. He never abandons them, as Samuel assured them, even when they had rejected the Lord by demanding a human king (1 Sa. 12:22). The stream of prophets never dries up, recalling the people to obedience and faith. Even in the most depressing times God is still there. Elijah thought that he was the only faithful Israelite left, but God told him otherwise (1 Ki. 19:14–18). Jerusalem lay in ruins for 140 years, until God's moment and God's person arrived, and bold, godly Nehemiah rebuilt it.

'Observing the Plan' means reading these histories with the covenant in mind and remembering that God's purpose is universal, and is not concerned with Israel alone. Sometimes this appears explicitly, although it is never far below the surface. Ruth, the Moabitess, is welcomed into Israel and becomes an ancestress of King David (Ru. 4:13–17). Ittai, the Gittite, was one of David's most faithful servants (2 Sa. 15:19–21). Naaman, an Aramean, became a worshipper of the God of Israel and was given permission to worship him without being circumcised, and outside Israel, in his own land (2 Ki. 5:17–19).

We, as Gentile believers at the end of the twentieth century, stand in exactly the same position as Ittai the Gittite and Naaman the Aramean, when we read these stories. We are looking in through a window at a life which is foreign to us, and yet to which we belong. We are not, and can never be, related to God under the terms of the old covenant as the Israelites were; and yet we do belong to him, just as they did, and we share the same human nature that made their relationship with him so stormy. We can learn much, therefore, both about the development of his Plan as it moved towards its climax in Jesus, and about how we should follow him in practice, in fellowship with the saints of the Old Testament who have gone before us.

All foods clean?

The relevance of Old Testament law

My wife and I read through Leviticus in our evening 'quiet time' shortly after we were married. We started at Genesis 1 on our wedding day, and so reached Leviticus before too long. But I must confess that, though we have now been married for twenty-two years, we have never been back to Leviticus! Partly, of course, the trouble was the time of day (or rather, night): Leviticus isn't recommended if you are beginning to doze anyway! We also made the mistake of reading it without any kind of study guide or commentary. But beyond these failures of method on our part, there was a further factor: what is the relevance of these old laws to us as Christians today? We couldn't get away from the feeling that, in the long run, they don't have much to say to us.

Some Bibles reinforce this feeling. I have an edition of the New English Bible produced for schools. Through the 'story' sections of Genesis and Exodus the text is printed in double columns on each page. But when it reaches the laws in Exodus, Leviticus and Numbers, the print becomes smaller and three columns of type are squeezed on to each page. There could hardly be a clearer signal that these parts are less important! But can this be right? After all, they still form part of the Bible. What right have we to regard any part of the Bible as less vital than another? And if they are just as important, should we in fact still obey the Old Testament laws today, strange though some of them seem?

Does Old Testament law apply to us?

Here are five sample passages from Leviticus, on which we can base our thinking about this question.

(A) All flying insects that walk on all fours are to be detestable to you. There are, however, some winged creatures that walk on all fours that you may eat: those that have jointed legs for hopping on the ground. Of these you may eat any kind of locust, katydid, cricket or grasshopper. But all other winged creatures that have four legs you are to detest.

(Lv. 11:20–23)

(B) The sin offering is to be slaughtered before the LORD in the place where the burnt offering is slaughtered; it is most holy. The priest who offers it shall eat it; it is to be eaten in a holy place, in the courtyard of the Tent of Meeting. Whatever touches any of the flesh will become holy, and if any of the blood is spattered on a garment, you must wash it in a holy place.

(Lv. 6:25–27)

(C) When you reap the harvest of your land, do not reap to the very edges of your field or gather the gleanings of your harvest. Do not go over your vineyard a second time or pick up the grapes that have fallen. Leave them for the poor and the alien. I am the LORD your God.

(Lv. 19:9–10)

(D) Do not seek revenge or bear a grudge against one of your people, but love your neighbour as yourself. I am the LORD.
Keep my decrees.
Do not mate different kinds of animals.
Do not plant your field with two kinds of seed.

Do not wear clothing woven of two kinds of material.

(Lv. 19:18–19)

(E) If a man or woman has a sore on the head or on the chin, the priest is to examine the sore, and if it appears to be more than skin deep and the hair in it is yellow and thin, the priest shall pronounce that person unclean. *(Lv. 13:29–30)*

We can immediately see the relevance of some of these laws. 'Love your neighbour as yourself' (D) is quoted on several occasions in the New Testament and underlined by Jesus himself. (Survey Mt. 5:43–44; 19:19; 22:39–40; Mk. 12:31, 33; Lk. 10:27; Rom. 13:9–10; Gal. 5:14; Ja. 2:8; and 1 Jn. 3:23, to get a sense of how important it is in the New Testament.) Similarly, the Ten Commandments are made vital for Christians in the New Testament (Mk. 10:17–19; Rom. 13:8–9; Eph. 6:2–3; 1 Tim. 1:8–11). They express something basic about God and about humanity which is universally true, regardless of time and place: this is what God is like and this is the way humankind should live.

But 'Love your neighbour as yourself' immediately precedes 'Do not mate different kinds of animals' (that is, 'Do not cross-breed your cattle'). Is this therefore just as important and authoritative for Christians? This would have radical implications for Christian farmers. And what about, 'Do not wear clothing woven of two kinds of material'? As I sit writing, I am wearing a jumper which is 80% acrylic and 20% nylon. I put it on this morning without thinking that I might be breaking God's holy law.

We begin to discover answers when we set these laws back into their original context and ask: what was the purpose of such regulations? When we discover this, we can see whether they have any relevance to us today and, if so, how. For instance, C could be interpreted as a law against 100% efficient combine harvesters. But would this be right? It was a humanitarian law aimed at benefiting the landless poor. But, in our society, there are more poor in the cities than in the countryside. We need to spot the purpose of the principle underlying the regulation – that the 'haves' must take action to meet the needs of the 'have nots' in the way they conduct their business. Then we can ask what application of the principle would be appropriate in our society today. The application could be very different, and might be different for each of us, depending on our situation.

In fact, it is not too difficult to handle the social laws, illustrated by C. Compared to the laws of ancient Egypt and Babylon, Old Testament law shows great concern for the underprivileged in society. Groups which were mercilessly exploited in other societies were specifically protected under Old Testament law, especially women and slaves. For instance, all slaves had to be released every seventh year, with their debts forgiven, and their former masters had to supply them with the provisions they would need in order to make a new start (Dt. 15:12–14). The reason for this amazingly liberal law then follows:

> Remember that you were slaves in Egypt and the LORD your God redeemed you. That is why I give you this command today. *(Dt. 15:15)*

The motivation for social care arises straight out of the Lord's love shown in his salvation of Israel from slavery. They are to imitate him in their corporate life. Exactly the same is true for us, although the precise application may differ: we have to 'be imitators of God . . . as dearly loved children and live a life of love, just as Christ loved us and gave himself up for us as a fragrant offering and sacrifice to God' (Eph. 5:1–2). The challenge is to work out exactly what we must do in order to 'be imitators of God' in our situation.

But it is harder to see how some of the other laws apply today. What about those against mixed breeding and types of cloth? And what about A and E above? These are examples of many laws devoted to distinguishing between 'clean' and 'unclean' foods and people.

With regard to E, it is especially important to note that these were not health regulations. Doubtless they had a good effect from a health point of view, because the people with skin infections or discharges were usually separated from everyone else. But this was not their purpose. The reason for the separation was that people with such diseases were regarded as ceremonially or ritually 'unclean', and therefore temporarily unfit to participate in worship and in the ordinary life of God's people. Today, they strike us as rather cruel – particularly the rule that people pronounced unclean had to wear torn clothes, go about with their hair dishevelled, wear a face-mask, call out 'Unclean! Unclean!' and live alone outside the camp (Lv. 13:45–56). How should we handle such regulations today?

Perhaps of even more concern are the laws against homosexual practices. 'If a man lies with a man as one lies with a woman, both of them have done what is detestable. They must be put to death; their blood will be on their own heads' (Lv. 20:13; see also Lv. 18:22; Dt. 23:17–18). Quite apart from the savagery of the penalty, there are many today who argue that this prohibition rests on ideas which we do not share, so that we should pension it off, along with the laws against mixed cloth and against cutting your beard (Lv. 19:27).

How do we answer these questions? For us as Christians, the vital clue lies in the relationship between the Old Testament and the New. We need to discover how the laws are handled in the New Testament, and then seek to handle them in the same way ourselves. But in order to understand what we find in the New Testament, we need to start in the Old, and ask what the purpose of all these laws was.

The purpose of Old Testament law

How did the laws fit into the Rescue Plan which God launched with his choice of Abraham and the nation descended from him? Some Christians think of the law as a kind of interlude in the Plan – in fact, a false way of salvation, which didn't work. They picture it as though God started with one way of salvation for humankind – the way of instruction and obedience to his will. But when that failed (because people were simply not able to obey him), he abandoned that method and introduced another, the way of faith in Jesus Christ. But this is mistaken. The law was never intended to be a means of climbing up to God by ourselves. Rather, it sets out the lifestyle appropriate for those who have already been saved.

The giving of the law follows God's rescue of Israel from Egypt. Just before giving Israel the Ten Commandments at Mount Sinai, the Lord tells them:

> I carried you on eagles' wings and brought you to myself. Now if you obey me fully and keep my covenant, then out of all nations you will be my treasured possession. Although the whole earth is mine, you will be for me a kingdom of priests and a holy nation. *(Ex. 19:4–6)*

God had already saved Israel and made them his; so he goes on to tell them how they should live now that they belong to him. The law that follows describes the lifestyle the 'holy nation' must adopt.

They must do this for a special reason: they are 'a kingdom of priests'. This idea of 'priesthood' gives us the key to unlock the purpose of the law. Priests mediate between God and humanity. In just the same way, Israel is meant to stand between God and the rest of the world, representing in vivid, visible form what it means to live in fellowship with the Creator. The fellowship was lost in Eden, and the world fell into disharmony and sin. But God seeks to bring the world back, and does so by choosing a people who will display what could have been – what was once, but was lost. In so doing, this people will actually be revealing the character and being of the God who made the world. The rest of the world is meant to be able to look at Israel and see what they could enjoy too. This means that Old Testament law has three purposes.

1. It underlines Israel's distinctiveness

Israel is a 'holy nation'. The basic meaning of 'holy' is 'separate, distinct, belonging to God'. Israel is different from the other nations of the world, because she is special to God. This is really the basic principle underlying all the different sorts of laws and regulations, as we shall see. All male Israelites had to accept the 'sign' of circumcision, to remind them constantly of their separation and distinctiveness (see Gn. 17:10–14; Ex. 22:29–30; Lv. 12:13).

2. It reveals God's character

This point follows on from the first. Israel is to be different from the nations, because God himself is different. 'You are to be holy to me because I, the LORD, am holy, and I have set you apart from the nations to be my own' (Lv. 20:26). In her very distinctiveness, Israel shows the world what God is like. Throughout Leviticus, the laws are interspersed with 'I am the LORD' or 'I am the LORD your God', underlining the point that these laws arise straight from the character of the Lord himself. In Leviticus 19, from which passages C and D are taken, this 'refrain' appears no fewer than fifteen times.

3. It shows the way to fellowship with God

The other nations could see that Israel's God lived among his people. The tabernacle in the centre of the nation was called the 'tent of meeting' (see passage B), because there God and his people met together. But the nations could also see that this was possible only because of the sacrifices that were offered there day and night. Israel shows how God deals with the sin which has ruined the world, so that sinners may live in harmony with him. And so at the heart of the law are regulations governing the sacrifices and the administration of the tabernacle.

These three reasons for the law correspond to the three distinctions within it which theologians used to make. It used to be fashionable to distinguish between

- *civil* laws, concerned with the practical administration of national life;
- *moral* laws, dealing with basic principles, like 'You shall not steal'; and
- *ceremonial* laws, regulating the sacrifices and the observance of purity.

This distinction was then used to help Christians handle the law. The theory was that the civil law is no longer applicable because it was relevant only for Israel, and the ceremonial law has been made unnecessary by Jesus, who is the full and final sacrifice for sin. Only the moral law is still applicable today.

This distinction is quite helpful, because clearly purpose 1 relates basically to the civil law, purpose 2 to the moral law, and purpose 3 to the ceremonial. But we need to be careful about it, for the Old Testament itself does not distinguish between them. Passage C, for instance, is a civil law. But it is immediately preceded in Leviticus 19 by a law concerning the proper eating of sacrificial meat – a ceremonial law. And it is immediately followed by some moral laws which remind us of the Ten Commandments: 'Do not steal. Do not lie. Do not deceive one another. Do not swear falsely by my name' (Lv. 19:11–12). Within the space of eight verses, all three types of law are mixed together without any sense of differing importance. This is because, at root, the three purposes all come together into a single aim: to shape a people who will show the world, by their lifestyle together, who God is and what it means to live in peace with him.

The law in the New Testament

Having looked at the purpose of the law in Old Testament

times, we need to see how the New Testament writers handled it. In fact, they too noticed these three purposes of Old Testament law and handled it differently in relation to each. In a nutshell, they affirmed the law in its basic revelation of God's character and concerns, but clearly believed that the coming of Jesus meant a radical change in relation to the law's other two purposes. It was not that God had gone back on his word, but that he had introduced a new direction into his Plan for the world, with far-reaching implications for our attitude to the old laws.

1. The law and God's character

The New Testament is eager to affirm that the law, along with the rest of the Old Testament, gives a true revelation of God's character and concerns. It is therefore basically binding on all who want to belong to him. Jesus tells the 'rich young ruler' that he must obey the Ten Commandments in order to gain eternal life (Mk. 10:17–19). Paul likewise lists four of the Ten Commandments, connects them with the law of neighbour-love, and tells the Christians in Rome that they must fulfil them (Rom. 13:8–10). Of course, the New Testament writers believed that God was supremely revealed in Jesus; but they saw no contradiction between the character of Jesus and the character of God as revealed in the Scriptures. They looked at the Scriptures with new eyes, therefore, as if they had suddenly been given 3D spectacles through which to view them – Jesus-spectacles.

It is helpful to use this as a key to unlock the law today. The question, 'Knowing God as we do through Jesus, what does this passage teach about him?' will reveal some of its meaning for us. For instance, looking at our five passages, we could say that passage A reveals God's detailed knowledge of his creation, and detailed concern for our obedience; passage B, his passion for holiness; passage C, his practical care for the poor; passage D, his deep concern that his people should love one another; and passage E, his concern for our physical health. Thus we can follow the lead of the New Testament writers and look to the law to understand more of God's character and concerns.

Sometimes we need background information to help us to apply this approach. For instance, the law against cutting the beard (Lv. 19:27) relates to pagan religious practices. The Israelites are not to look as though they happily associate themselves with pagan religion. God is concerned about the message we give by the way we dress.

The situation is more complicated, however, when we turn to the other two purposes of the law: those of underlining Israel's distinctiveness as God's people, and revealing the means of fellowship with a holy God.

2. The law and distinctiveness

Let us take the example of the food laws (passage A). These were a vivid way of making God's Old Testament people distinct and different from the nations round about. Here is another important passage:

> You must not live according to the customs of the nations . . . I am the LORD your God, who has set you apart from the nations.
>
> You must therefore make a distinction between clean and unclean animals and between unclean and clean birds. Do not defile yourselves by any animal or bird or anything that moves along the ground – those which I have set apart as unclean for you. You are to be holy to me because I, the LORD, am holy . . .   *(Lv. 20:23–26)*

The 'unclean' animals were set apart just as Israel had been, so that the distinction between the animals they could eat, and those they could not, mirrored the distinction between Israel and the other nations. This is the reason, too, for those strange laws about not mixing different breeds, crops and types of cloth (passage D): the Israelites were surrounded in everyday life with reminders of the profound principle upon which their whole existence rested. Like their clothes, their crops and their cattle, the Israelites had to be special, unmixed, 'holy'. The regulations about ritual purity (E) had the same effect. Daily, they had to avoid contact with people who were ritually unclean and, if they themselves became unclean, they had to undergo various washings (of themselves and of their clothes) in order to be restored to full fellowship within the community (see Lv. 15:4–12). The principle of separation was written deeply into their daily life together.

When we come over to the New Testament, we find an enormous change. Israel's distinctiveness is completely abolished. The boundaries of God's people are stretched wide; all and sundry are invited in, regardless of national origin or background. Paul fought battles over this; it was not an easy idea for Jewish Christians to accept. Many continued to observe the food laws as Christians, and some of them felt passionately that Gentile converts ought to be circumcised and brought under the yoke of the law as well. (See Acts 15:1, 10. This issue underlies Paul's letters to the Romans and the Galatians.) Paul was happy for Jewish Christians to go on observing the law if they wanted to, but as far as his Gentile converts were concerned he felt that the whole truth of the gospel was being overturned by the demand that they should be circumcised. He believed that God was creating a new people, made out of Jews and Gentiles without distinction. So when Peter withdrew with the Jewish Christians from the mixed fellowship at Antioch, because they suddenly had a fit of scruples about the food laws, Paul had a public showdown with him (Gal. 2:11–21). 'They were not acting in line with the truth of the gospel' (verse 14).

Paul was right. Jesus had already made it clear that the barriers were to come down. In fact, he turned the Old Testament understanding of 'clean and unclean' on its head. When he stretched out his hand to touch the leper (Mk. 1:41), he was not just vividly showing the man sympathy. He was breaking the purity regulations! According to the law, he should have been made 'unclean' by the contact – and then he would have become a potential source of uncleanness for all who came into contact with him (Lv. 5:2–3). But the effect went the other way. The leper said to Jesus, 'If you are willing, you can make me clean.'

'I am willing,' he said. 'Be clean!' (Mk. 1:40–41).

Later, we discover that Jesus intended to do away with these laws. In Mark 7 he denounces the Pharisees for seeking perfect ritual purity at the expense of real obedience to God (Mk. 7:5–13). Then he goes further, deliberately abolishing the distinction between clean and unclean foods. He tells his disciples that

> nothing that enters a person from the outside can make that person 'unclean' . . . What defiles human beings is what comes out of them. For from within, out of the heart, come evil thoughts, sexual immorality, theft, murder, adultery, greed . . .   *(Mk. 7:18, 20–22, my translation)*

Mark adds the perceptive and revolutionary comment in brackets, 'thus Jesus made all foods "clean" ' (7:19). Then he tells the story of the Syro-Phoenician woman (7:24–30), a Gentile who would previously have been regarded as 'unclean' by all law-abiding Jews, but who now finds that the Messiah is her saviour, too.

Although Jesus did not minister much to Gentiles, and remained largely within the borders of Israel, his vision was clearly for a worldwide people of God. Gentiles like this woman would be drawn into it, along with other outcasts like the leper, who had effectively been excluded from the community of God's people. Abolishing the food and purity laws confirmed that it was God's plan to draw in the Gentiles. (For other places where we see Jesus drawing Gentiles into the kingdom or speaking of it, see Mt. 8:10–12; 10:18–20; 21:42–44; 24:14; 28:18–20; Jn. 10:14–16; 12:20–32; 17:18–23. There are many more places which illustrate the breaking down of other barriers erected by the law.)

Abolishing the laws was the sign that their purpose had been fulfilled. They had been given in order to make Israel distinct, so that the other nations would see the Creator in his special people, and be attracted to him. But with the coming of Jesus, who is the perfect revelation of God, two things happened. First, Israel's role as revealer was no longer needed; and secondly, that worldwide people is now being formed, simply through faith in the Messiah.

'People are not set right with God by observing rules and regulations, but by faith in Jesus Christ,' declared Paul (*cf.* Gal. 2:16). The food laws and all the other regulations that made Israel distinct were not an end in themselves. They were simply meant to point ahead to the coming of 'the holy one of God', the Messiah.

Further light is shed on this in John 13:1–17, where Jesus undertook the task of washing his disciples' feet before their last supper together. At every other Passover meal being held that night, such washing had no more than a ritual significance, making sure that everyone was properly 'clean' for the meal. But Jesus made it an act of service that foreshadowed his death for the disciples, and a picture of the cleansing and forgiveness which he would give them – something not just external, but touching their deepest need. After the meal, he told them, 'You are already clean because of the word I have spoken to you' (Jn. 15:3). He used the ritual to picture a spiritual cleansing available through his teaching and through his death, and not through the law.

How do we know whether or not a particular law is a 'distinctiveness' law now set aside for Christians? There are some disputed cases. The two most important are the Sabbath laws, and the laws against homosexuality mentioned above. The command to 'remember the Sabbath day, to keep it holy' is actually one of the Ten Commandments (Ex. 20:8; Dt. 5:12). Shouldn't we then keep it as carefully as 'You shall not murder'? On the other hand, were the laws against homosexual practices simply another way in which Israel was meant to be marked as different from the nations around?

We need to apply the principle of looking at these laws through the spectacles of the New Testament. When we do this, we discover some remarkable things. The first Christians did not keep the Sabbath! They were probably encouraged in this by Jesus himself (Mk. 2:23–28). Nowhere does Paul encourage his Gentile converts to take up the habit of Sabbath observance. Instead, all Christians adopted the new practice of marking the first day of the week, rather than the seventh, as a focus of their worship (Acts 20:7; 1 Cor. 16:2), clearly because this was the day of Jesus' resurrection (Mt. 28:1). It came to be known as the 'Lord's Day' (Rev. 1:10). Though one of the Ten Commandments, Sabbath observance was treated like the food laws – a distinctive feature of Israel's life which is not to mark out the followers of Jesus Christ. They are marked in other ways.

And of course the prohibition of homosexual practices was also a distinctive feature of Israel's life. In other societies, there were few strong feelings about homosexual activity; generally, nobody objected. So Israel was again marked as different. But in this case, the spectacles of the New Testament reveal something different. This prohibition is not blended out of the picture, like Sabbath observance, but highlighted in even stronger colours. In Romans 1:24–27, 1 Corinthians 6:9–10 and 1 Timothy 1:10 Paul condemns homosexual practices much more strongly than anything in the Old Testament.

Why is there this difference? Clearly, Sabbath observance touches something particular to Israel, but homosexuality touches something particular to humankind: our whole sexual make-up, constituted by God in creation, is offended by homosexual acts. And so Christians are called to reaffirm the teaching of the Old Testament here. In both cases, the New Testament helps us to handle the Old.

3. The law and fellowship with God

As with the laws of 'distinctiveness', we need to be guided by the way the laws of sacrifice are handled in the New Testament.

Passage B is a sample of the laws governing the sacrifices. The fact that the Israelites were commanded by God to sacrifice animals is something that we might find hard to understand. Again, we must understand the purpose of these sacrifices. Notice how often the word 'holy' is used in passage B. It is applied to the offering, to the place where the offering is made, and to anything in contact with the sacrificial meat. As the 'holy nation', Israel is allowed to draw near to the Lord, the holy God. But she can do so only through blood, because death is the inevitable consequence of sin in this world. The sacrificial system opens the door to fellowship with God by providing a means whereby that death is borne, not by the sinner, but by an animal sacrificed in the sinner's place.

But even though God lived among Israel, he remained 'holy', distinct, separate – in fact, unapproachable. Sinners could go to the 'Tent of Meeting' with the sacrifices and receive an assurance of forgiveness as they saw the blood spilt – and yet they knew they could never enter the 'Most Holy Place', where God actually was. This was a room at the centre of the tabernacle (and later at the centre of the temple), which only the high priest was allowed to enter, once a year, on the Day of Atonement. The regulations governing the Day of Atonement are described in Leviticus 16. It had two purposes: dealing with all the forgotten or unnoticed sins of the past year, and making atonement for the priests themselves, who were so crucial for the whole system. The entry of the high priest into the Most Holy Place showed that he himself was acceptable to God, and that the sacrificial system was working for the people as a whole.

But – just one person, just once a year! 'Tent of Meeting' was a strange name for the tabernacle. The whole system was meant to tell the world how humankind may be reconciled to God, and yet actually God remained alone, in isolated holiness in the Most Holy Place.

According to the book of Hebrews, this strict separation within the tabernacle is a picture of the separation between earth and the real 'Most Holy Place', heaven itself, where God truly dwells (Heb. 9:1–12). The high priest could never enter that place, and this was proof that the sacrifices he offered were simply not effective. But Jesus has entered the heavenly 'Most Holy Place'. 'Christ did not enter a physical sanctuary, one which merely symbolizes the true sanctuary, but he entered heaven itself, to appear now before God on our behalf . . . he appeared once for all, at the end of the ages, to do away with sin by the sacrifice of himself' (Heb. 9:24, 26, my translation).

Hebrews does not refer to the story in Matthew 27:51, which tells how, when Jesus died, 'the curtain of the temple was torn in two from top to bottom'. But it fits, theologically. This curtain hung before the Most Holy Place, barring the way into God's presence. It was destroyed to show that the separation from God which was built into Old Testament religion has been destroyed through the death of Jesus. Now we may be truly reconciled to God.

Jesus turns out to be the meaning behind the Old Testament rituals. He has held a once-for-all day of atonement for the whole world. Just as the Old Testament ceremony was meant to cover the sins of the past year, particularly the ones committed in ignorance, so Jesus' atonement looks back, not just over one year, but over the whole of history, past and future. In the past, no forgiveness was possible through the animal sacrifices themselves, only through what they pictured: the final, glorious sacrifice of Jesus himself. Those who offered sacrifices in faith that God would forgive them were justified by faith, not by the death of the animals. And for the future, we say with confidence: no sin is so great that Jesus' death cannot cover it. We need do no more.

Applying the laws today

We have thought about the principles involved in applying Old Testament laws to our lives as Christians. We shall finish this chapter with some more detailed comments under the same three headings.

1. The law and God's concerns today

We have already noted that each of our five passages reveals something about God's character or concerns. For instance, many of the laws, like those in Leviticus 19:9–10 (C), reveal God's concern for the poor. In ancient societies, the poor were dependent upon the thoughtfulness and care of the richer. God encourages this! We see this particular law, about not harvesting right to the edge of the field, in action in the book of Ruth (2:2 onwards). And it is interesting that this care extended beyond the immediate social group; the 'alien' had to be included. The message for us is clear, because this reveals something about the character of God himself. Christians really must have a 'bias towards the poor', and not just towards our own society. In a world plagued by the grossest inequalities, Christians should be at the forefront of those who reach out to the poor and the marginalized.

2. The 'distinctiveness' laws today

In the light of the New Testament's reinterpretation of the 'distinctiveness' laws, we can see three ways in which they make claims on us today.

First, they tell us to be *holy*. Being 'set apart' for God had an effect on every moment of the Israelites' lives: what they wore, what they ate, even what they sat on (see Lv. 15:6). We, too, need to take minute care in following the Lord Jesus. Every tiny part of our lives is his, and every second of our time – because we belong to him totally, just as ancient Israel did. Laws like those in passage D are saying, 'You must not try to mix oil with water! The Israelites could not, for instance, mix loving their neighbours with seeking revenge against them; and to remind them of this, God told them to dress in clothes of unmixed cloth and to plant unmixed crops in their fields. Applying this to ourselves, we can be reminded of Jesus' words, 'No-one can serve two masters . . . You cannot serve both God and Money' (Mt. 6:24). And we can share Paul's concern for the Corinthians:

'I am afraid in case your thoughts will be diverted from the single-mindedness and purity Christ requires!' (2 Cor. 11:3, my translation).

God no longer requires us to wear unmixed cloth, but the principle is still the same. We cannot be half in love with him and half in love with the world. James expresses this principle vividly in James 4:4: 'You adulterous people, don't you know that friendship with the world is hatred towards God?' Then he goes on to apply this to the way some business people conduct their affairs without reference to God's plans for them (4:13–17). The influence of the world can be very subtle, shaping our sense of 'normal life' in a way that pulls us perhaps miles from God's will for us.

Secondly, God's laws call us to be *different*. The surrounding nations were left in no doubt: because of their God, the Israelites had to live a very different lifestyle. Which distinctive marks reveal to the world at large that we are Christians? We could point to big things, like the vibrancy of our worship and the depth of our love for each other. But perhaps it would be more appropriate to ask about the little things which should mark us out as well. The distinction between types of insect that the Israelites could or could not eat (passage A) gave quite a dramatic message to the world around, precisely because it was such a tiny detail. It said that Israel's devotion to God touches every smallest action, every shortest moment.

Is that the unspoken message we give about our love for Christ?

Thirdly, God's laws instruct us to be *clean*. The laws of 'distinctiveness' point us to the cleansing available through Jesus. As we saw above, the emphasis on physical cleansing in the purity regulations has, in the New Testament, been turned into an emphasis on spiritual cleansing. The author of Hebrews expresses this thought as follows:

When the blood of goats and bulls and the ashes of a heifer were sprinkled on those who were ceremonially unclean, they were sanctified and made pure in flesh. How much more, then, will the blood of Christ, who through the eternal Spirit offered himself unblemished to God, make us pure in conscience from acts that lead to death, so that we may serve the living God! *(Heb. 9:13–14, my translation)*

This is the main theme of the book of Hebrews. It describes the religion of the Old Testament, with its priests and tabernacle and sacrifices, and shows how these were all a massive visual aid, pointing forward to Jesus and enabling us to understand him properly. But as they teach us about him, they challenge us about our worship and lifestyle, as well – or, to use Hebrews' words, about our conscience and our service. The two go together. The priests had elaborate rituals to perform at set times, and in many ways this is much easier! Instead, we have to serve the Lord with pure hearts and clean consciences, because that is what Jesus has provided and now makes possible for us, moment by moment. This is challenging.

3. The laws of sacrifice today

What will these laws teach us today if we let the New Testament guide us? Four things.

The first is *the seriousness of sin*. The sacrifices show so vividly that sin means death. There is no way around it: either the sinner must die or someone else must bear the penalty. We must not trivialize the holiness of God. He cannot turn a blind eye to sin.

Secondly, *God provides the answer*. The sacrifices were God's gift to Israel because he did not want them to remain lost in sin and death. In the long run, this meant that 'he loved us and sent his Son as an atoning sacrifice for our sins' (1 Jn. 4:10); he gives a far greater gift.

Thirdly, we have a *'place' of forgiveness*. The Israelites had to go to the tabernacle or temple in order to offer their sacrifices. We too go to a 'place', but it is not a physical location. Jesus is for us the place of atonement, and we go to him by faith. He is our temple (Jn. 2:19–21), the place where atonement is made; and, joined to him, we ourselves become the temple (1 Cor. 3:16, Eph. 2:14–22), the place where worship is offered.

Finally, the sacrifices speak of the cost of forgiveness. It was not a light matter for an Israelite to sacrifice a precious animal to God. And it had to be one of the best: he could not palm God off with a sick animal of no commercial value (Dt. 17:1). Repentance was very real and very costly.

God also gave his best: his only Son. It cost him a tremendous amount to forgive us. When we understand this, we see in perspective the cost of the sacrifice we must make in response. Repentance can mean nothing less than offering ourselves to God, body and soul, as living sacrifices (Rom. 12:1–2). We cannot palm God off either, but must give him our best.

'An orderly account for you'

Reading the gospels

Date: AD 196. Place: the accessions room of the huge library in Alexandria, Egypt. An elderly librarian sits thumbing through a slim volume which has just been donated to the library. He has the job of deciding how it should be catalogued, and he isn't finding it easy. Its title could hardly be plainer, and hardly more puzzling: 'Good News according to Mark'.

'Who is this Mark? Fancy publishing a book under a forename only,' muses the librarian, 'without any further names or places mentioned. And what is this "good news"?'

As he skims through the book (it's so short!), he realizes it is a kind of biography of one 'Jesus'. 'Ah! That's the answer. I can classify this under "Biography".

'But it is a very strange biography. There is nothing about the birth or childhood of this "Jesus". And it doesn't concentrate on extolling the moral virtues of its subject, like the other biographies we have. The book seems to settle down to narrating a string of extraordinary miracles performed by Jesus. Ah! Perhaps that's it. I could put this in the "Mighty Deeds" section, with all the other books that record the heroic doings of some great figure. We have lots of those. But hold on! This book seems to devote disproportionate space – yes, about a third of its length – to the *death* of the subject! Hardly a heroic deed . . .

'Well, what about "Memoirs"? We have a large section full of appreciative memoirs of great figures, written by their disciples to preserve their memory. I could put this with them. But there are hardly any records of the teaching of this 'Jesus' here. And not only is it short, it's so incomplete! Who on earth wrote this thing? He has ruined my classification system! This kind of rubbish won't last, anyway. I'll put it under "Ephemera".'

I have borrowed the idea for this imaginary librarian from Professor Christopher Evans. There really was nothing exactly like the gospels in the ancient world. We have become used to them, so they do not puzzle us. But what kind of books are the 'gospels'? They are clearly not ordinary biographies, written in order to preserve a memory from dying out, because they presuppose an extensive background knowledge in their readers. For instance, Mark assumes that his readers will already know where Jesus lived (in Palestine) and who his parents were (Mk. 6:3). John similarly assumes that his readers will know that Jesus was born in Bethlehem (Jn. 7:42). Beyond these details, the gospels assume that their readers will be happy with something so short, and will not be brimming over with questions, wanting to know more. Why do they make this assumption?

We could put the same question another way by asking why Matthew, Mark and Luke have so much material in common with each other. All but twenty-two verses of Mark also appear in Matthew and Luke! Scholars agonize about 'who used whom', and in view of this statistic it is not surprising that the usual answer is, 'Matthew and Luke used Mark.' But there seems to have been no shortage of material. John says explicitly that Jesus did far more than he recorded in his gospel (Jn. 20:30; 21:25). So why this strange overlap? In addition, about another 23% of Matthew also appears in Luke. Why is this? We are faced with two puzzles: why did they select the same things? And why are they so short?

Size and purpose

We need to seek answers to these questions, because only then shall we be able to work out right principles for reading and interpreting the gospels. The puzzle of their length is easier to handle. Luke's is the longest gospel (1,150 verses, 81 more than Matthew), and is about the maximum length which could conveniently be fitted on to a scroll. The 'book' (that is, sheets of paper folded and stitched together at the fold) was probably invented early in the second century: until then the scroll was the form of book-production used throughout the Graeco-Roman world. Luke's gospel would produce a scroll about 32 ft (10 metres) long, according to Professor Bruce Metzger, and anything longer would be very cumbersome. It looks as though Luke, at any rate, wanted to keep his account of Jesus within that size, perhaps partly because he intended to produce a second volume (slightly shorter at 1,005 verses), covering the life of the first Christians.

But Mark is barely half the length of Luke (662 verses). He was clearly not limited by this book-production factor. What then? Here another factor appears, which applies in fact to all four gospels. John tells us that he selected the material for inclusion in his gospel to match his precise purpose in writing:

> Jesus did many other signs before his disciples, which are not written in this book. But these were written so that you might believe that Jesus is the Christ, the Son of God, and that believing you might have life in his name.
>
> *(Jn. 20:30–31, my translation)*

John here reveals something of the careful crafting which has gone into his writing. 'These were written' means both 'These were chosen so that . . .' and 'I have carefully written the story so that . . .' Scholars debate who the 'you' are, to whom John addressed his gospel. Are they non-Christian Jews? Or any kind of unbeliever? Or are they Christians – perhaps members of

John's own church? Or Christians with wrong ideas about Jesus? Whatever the answer, John's selectivity was shaped by his purpose.

It is likely that the other gospel-writers also wrote with a particular purpose, and this might help to explain both their length and the overlap between them.

Mark

There is an ancient tradition that Mark's gospel was based on the preaching and teaching of Peter and was written for the church in Rome, possibly just after Peter's death. We learn from Papias, Bishop of Hierapolis in about AD 120, that he himself had been taught that Mark acted as Peter's 'interpreter' and wrote down a full account of Peter's memories of Jesus. We can well imagine that Peter's preaching would have focused on the stories and sayings of Jesus which Peter regarded as either most typical or most helpful for his hearers, and so might not have been very extensive. And probably Mark had his own purposes, too. There is a strong and early tradition that both Peter and Paul died in Nero's persecution of the Christians in Rome, which broke out in AD 65. The church there faced terrible suffering and loss. If Mark wrote in the aftermath of this experience, it would help explain his emphasis on the cost of discipleship and the sufferings of Jesus.

Anything based on Peter's teaching would have had a ready audience wherever he had ministered, however, so even if Mark had a more limited aim to start with, his gospel will have quickly been valued elsewhere. In the closing decades of the first century, many different persecuted churches would have found comfort from Mark's particular emphases.

Matthew

Papias also reports the early tradition that Matthew wrote down 'Jesus' sayings' originally in Aramaic. The gospel as we now have it is of course in Greek, and shows no signs of having been translated from Aramaic. And if Matthew used Mark's

(Greek) gospel, as seems likely, then our version of Matthew's gospel must also have been written in Greek. But there could have been a prior Aramaic edition of Matthew, perhaps especially compiled for the Jewish churches of Syria and Judea, where Aramaic was widely spoken. Matthew certainly has a special interest in the Old Testament and in Jesus' fulfilment of prophecy, which might point to a particular concern for Jewish Christians.

Comparing his with the other gospels, some scholars have suggested that he wrote with the needs of worship leaders or of young Christians especially in mind. These needs would have been widely felt in the church – the need to have materials in a form suitable for use in public worship, and to supply the need of new Christians for instruction in basic Christian teaching. Matthew groups the teaching of Jesus into great blocks in his gospel (chapters 5 – 7, 10, 13, 18, 23 – 25), and these would satisfy both needs, providing material which could easily be used either in worship or in instruction.

Mark does not include much of Jesus' teaching. So perhaps we can imagine something like this:

- Matthew first produces an Aramaic record of Jesus' 'sayings'.
- Then he comes across Mark's gospel, the record of Peter's memories, and realizes that it complements his sayings-gospel beautifully.
- So he produces a totally revised gospel, this time in Greek so as to appeal to a wider audience, incorporating his records of Jesus' teaching into a narrative framework supplied by Mark.

This is probably a greatly oversimplified picture of what happened, but it might be true in essence.

Luke

Luke gives us a fascinating insight into his purposes in his unique preface (Lk. 1:1–4), which we shall examine below. He is more independent of Matthew and Mark than they are of each other; almost exactly 50% of his gospel is his alone. In particular, there is a long section in the middle (Lk. 9:51–19:27), known as Luke's 'travel narrative' because Jesus is travelling to Jerusalem throughout this section, in which nearly all the material is only in Luke. In addition, he contains less of Mark than Matthew does (452 of Mark's 662 verses), and about 100 of these verses are reworded or combined with other material, and not reproduced exactly.

Even though he seems relatively independent, scholars have been fascinated by the fact that (like Matthew) Luke still basically follows the order of events recorded in Mark, simply slotting his 'new' material into Mark's. What was Luke up to? We can gain insight into his purpose, and at the same time into this difficult question of the overlap between the gospels, if we take a special look at his preface.

Gospel origins: Luke's testimony

Luke's little preface (1:1–4) serves as an introduction to both his volumes (Luke and Acts):

> Seeing that many have undertaken to draw up an account of the things fulfilled among us – drawing on the material handed down to us by those who from the first became eyewitnesses and servants of the word – I decided that I too would write an orderly account for you, most excellent Theophilus, based on painstaking and original research, so that you might know the certainty of the things you have been taught. *(my translation)*

There are three things to note about what he says here.

1. Luke is one of 'us'

The events he writes about took place 'among us', and the information about them was handed down 'to us'. The group implied by this 'us' is clearly the early Christian church. The first 'us' refers to the very first Christians, who were eyewitnesses of the ministry of Jesus. The second 'us' are people like Luke who were dependent upon the testimony of the first group. But he does not distinguish sharply between these two groups; they are all 'us'. There is a sense of fellowship here, the community of those who were joined to each other by a common love for Christ and a desire to worship him.

Within this group there was already widespread knowledge of Christ, so this focuses our question about the *purpose* of the gospels. Clearly, they were meant first and foremost to serve the needs of 'us', the believing and worshipping group among whom these 'things were fulfilled'. But this group has fuzzy borders. We do not know who Theophilus, Luke's literary patron, was. But plainly he is hovering on the fringes of the church; he has already learned a certain amount and Luke wants him to develop his knowledge, so he dedicates his gospel to him, and to all like him. Within the setting of 'us', the believing community, Theophilus' further questions will be answered and Luke's gospel will be set alongside the letters and the wider ministry of the apostles.

2. There were many previous accounts of Jesus' ministry

Sadly, none of the many previous accounts of Jesus' ministry has survived. Undoubtedly, the reason for this is that they were displaced by our gospels. People no longer felt the need for them, now that they had Matthew and Co. This suggests that there was a clear, qualitative difference between these 'many' earlier accounts, and our four gospels. We have to use a little imagination to work out what this difference was.

We can imagine that the earliest Christians were intensely interested in the stories of Jesus' ministry and teaching. Luke's prominent mention of 'eyewitnesses and servants of the word' suggests that people who could speak authoritatively and accurately about Jesus were in demand. Many people had cherished memories of what Jesus had said and done (see Jn.

21:25), and we can imagine the leading teachers, like Peter, forming their own mental or written collections of favourite stories for use on the preaching trail. Various written collections were made, presumably in different places and for different purposes. Certain stories would have been especially useful for communicating a particular feature of Jesus' teaching, or for vividly conveying a sense of his person and presence. Other stories would begin to drop out of regular public use. Memories would begin to vary from place to place, as different stories or collections came to be associated with particular teachers or churches. And as the church expanded and the same stories were retold in different settings, so the style and vocabulary of the retelling would vary.

We can see indications of this variety in our gospels. Even though Matthew, Mark and Luke have so much material in common, the precise wording often differs, sometimes in ways that makes a clear change in the sense. For instance, in Luke 15:3–7 the parable of the lost sheep illustrates God's love for the outcasts of society – the 'tax-collectors and sinners' whom Jesus addresses there. But in Matthew 18:12–14 the same parable is told differently, and has a different message. It appears in a passage dealing with relationships within 'the church', and teaches love for children within the Christian fellowship. Of course, Jesus teaches love for children elsewhere, and he himself may have reapplied the parable of the lost sheep in this way. But Matthew may be reflecting the way the telling of the parable varied in the church.

We must also bear in mind the change of language which took place during the period to which Luke refers here. Jesus probably taught largely in Aramaic, and the earliest Christians (the first 'us') were Aramaic-speaking. But by the time of the gospels the church had become solidly Greek-speaking; it needed to, as the gospel spread. This need for translation of the stories would have simply proliferated the number of accounts and records, and thus made variations even more possible.

Someone like Theophilus would therefore have been faced

with a bewildering variety of records and memories of Jesus. Did he perhaps comment to his friend Luke that he did not know which Jesus to believe in – the Jesus as remembered in Jerusalem, or in Antioch, or in Rome, or in Ephesus? We can certainly imagine that, as the church grew, so the need of clear, reliable, universally recognized accounts of Jesus was felt.

3. Luke claims order and certainty for his gospel

When Luke describes his account as 'orderly' and 'certain', he probably implies a contrast with the earlier accounts. They were not 'orderly', and therefore not 'certain'. Both words tell us a lot about his intention. 'Orderly' has two shades of meaning.

- ▶ It claims something, first, about the *quality* of Luke's work: it is accurate, reflecting the very careful research that Luke undertook prior to writing, and the care he took to record events in their right 'order' – although Luke is probably not claiming strict chronological order.
- ▶ And it says something, secondly, about the *presentation* of Luke's work: he has composed it carefully to include all the relevant material and exclude the irrelevant, so that each item contributes to an 'ordered' whole. We shall think further about this later.

Luke wants to convey to Theophilus the 'certainty' or 'truth' about the stories he has heard; that is, both assurance of their reliability, and insight into their significance. (The Greek word translated 'know' means 'know and understand'.) Theophilus has already received some information about Jesus. Luke wants to lead him to a well-founded and confident understanding. He was clearly aware that, as a historian, he was not merely passing on the past, like a tape being replayed. He felt the responsibility that rests on all historians, to enable their readers to enter into the real meaning of what they record. He wanted Theophilus – and other readers, too – to grasp that meaning, the 'truth' about Jesus.

A clear picture emerges. Luke thought of his task as bringing order out of chaos. An orderly account would help Theophilus to see the certainty and truth at the heart of what must have looked like a rather disordered movement. Instead of a jumble of unconnected stories and sayings, circulating around the various churches and being retold in ever more widely varying ways, he wants to give us an ordered, clear, connected account, which both gets the facts right, and leads us to understand them properly.

All four gospels seem to have this origin and purpose. They seek to show us the essence of Jesus, by the judicious selection and arrangement of materials which had proved themselves in the experience of Christians to date. Undoubtedly, this partly explains the overlap; amid all the variety, certain stories had become particularly popular, and certain sayings and parables were specially loved. By their overlap, the gospels affirm the reliability of these memories.

But of course the question arises: are they right? For all that Luke claims to rest his gospel on accurate research, can we trust him and the other three? This is obviously a question of vital importance for Christians, particularly since the reliability of the gospels has been widely challenged, within the church as well as outside it. Can we claim that we can meet the real Jesus in the pages of the gospels? If not, then he must remain essentially unknown, and the faith of Christians today cannot reach further back than the faith of the first Christians. Is that in fact what the gospels give us: the first Christians' developed picture of a Jesus who in fact was very different?

The challenge

This challenge to the gospels' reliability rests on four inter-linked arguments.

First, Luke claims to have conducted careful research, but apparently relied quite heavily on Mark, possibly also on Matthew, in writing his gospel. If they are among the 'many' to whom he refers in his preface, then he cannot be more reliable than they. If they had already got it wrong, he could not avoid perpetuating their mistakes.

Secondly, the gospels' reliability is further called into question when we ask what happened in the period before they wrote. Mark's is usually regarded as the earliest, and if the connection with Peter is correct, then he wrote some thirty-five years after the death and resurrection of Jesus. What was happening to the memories of Jesus during this period? I described it above as a period of growing chaos, into which Luke sought to bring order. But how great was this chaos? Had the diversity become so great that none of the gospel writers stood any chance of doing a good job, whatever their claim?

Many scholars have indeed argued that the first Christians were not interested in preserving their memories of Jesus accurately, but freely adapted and added to the gospel materials so that we can no longer tell what is original and what is not. Some have linked this to the ministry of prophets in the early church: when a prophet spoke in the name of Christ, these new 'sayings' were added to the gospel traditions alongside the memories of Jesus, and the distinction between them was quickly lost.

Thirdly, at first sight this picture seems to be confirmed when we look at John's gospel. Once again, there is fairly reliable evidence that John's was the last gospel to be written. The picture of Jesus it presents is so different from the other three gospels that many scholars regard it more as a collection of meditations or sermons than as a work of history. For instance, in John Jesus performs no exorcisms (contrast Lk. 13:32), tells no parables (contrast Mk. 4:34), proclaims his identity openly (contrast Mk. 3:12; 8:30), and gives extended teaching in a style identical with John's own style. Here we see (scholars argue) the end of a long process in which the stories of Jesus have been mulled over and reshaped so thoroughly that the real, historical Jesus has virtually vanished and all we have left is what John believed about him.

Fourthly, what about the other gospels? The final stage in this argument is to point out how Matthew, Mark and Luke are no more trustworthy than John. Each has contributed to this process of degeneration by adapting the stories and sayings in line with his own interests. Mark, for instance, is especially interested in the theme of faith, and in showing how light slowly dawned on the disciples. But when Matthew records the same stories as Mark, he tells them in a way that brings his own special interests to the fore: the fulfilment of prophecy, for instance, or the practical obedience Jesus requires from his followers. Similarly, Luke does not scruple to move the story of Jesus' rejection at Nazareth to the very beginning of his ministry (Lk. 4:16–29), and tells the story much more fully than Mark (6:1–6), because that way he can introduce some of his favourite themes: Jesus' ministry to the poor, fulfilment of prophecy, anointing with the Spirit, rejection by the Jews and outreach to the Gentiles. So (we are told) the gospel writers were just interested in getting their own ideas across and were using a historical form simply as a convenient platform. Various factors in their situation, or that of their readers, created their particular interests, and they shaped their material to suit.

Recently this attack on the reliability of the gospels has been sharpened by the so-called 'Jesus Seminar', a group of largely American scholars who have committed themselves to 'the search for the authentic words of Jesus' (the title of one of their books). A vigorous publishing programme has meant that their work has received wide publicity, especially in the United States; but the ripples have been felt worldwide. Some eighty scholars belong to the Jesus Seminar, and they have invented a method of voting on the various sayings of Jesus so as to grade the likelihood that Jesus said them or not. The result is a series of 'red-letter' editions of the gospels, in which the authentic sayings are highlighted in red. But sadly it turns out that, according to the Seminar, only 18% of the sayings attributed to Jesus were certainly said by him! All the rest fall into three other categories, 'probably authentic', 'probably unauthentic' and 'certainly unauthentic'.

The Jesus Seminar is convinced that our interests are very different from those of the early church. Whereas we are very concerned to know how reliable the gospels are, apparently the first Christians were not too bothered. They allowed the traditions to develop and expand until certainty became impossible.

How true is this picture?

Responding to the challenge

We can say several things directly about the Jesus Seminar, and then several things more generally about the problem.

The Jesus Seminar . . .

First, the Seminar is by no means representative of scholarship generally. It was set up to represent and propagate a particular viewpoint. Of course, that does not necessarily mean that it is wrong, but it is important to be aware that there are many scholars who take a much more positive view.

Secondly, the methods employed to determine authenticity are clearly vital. How valid are they? A fishing-net with large mesh could lead you to conclude that there are no fish out there in the bay, whereas in fact they all got away through the holes. Something similar has happened with the Jesus Seminar, through an over-reliance on what is called 'the criterion of dissimilarity'. The argument runs likes this. We can regard as authentic those sayings which reveal attitudes or ideas not shared either by the early church, or by first-century Jews generally. In such cases, it is clear that the saying would not have come from these other sources, and so must have come from Jesus. There is nothing wrong with this as an argument, but the mesh is too wide to catch very many fish, because it automatically discounts all sayings in which Jesus expresses attitudes or ideas which he shared with the early church or with other Jews! It must surely be expected that his disciples would adopt his teaching; but this criterion recognizes as authentic only the bits of his teaching which his disciples did *not* follow!

Prominent use of the 'criterion of dissimilarity', therefore, will certainly point to a basically sceptical attitude towards the early church. It reveals a fundamental assumption that the first Christians quickly distorted the authentic traditions. But this assumption does not fit the evidence, as we shall see.

Thirdly, the Jesus Seminar has gone out on a scholarly limb by the prominent use they make of the apocryphal *Gospel of Thomas*. This is a late collection of sayings of Jesus, used by a heretical Gnostic group in the late second century. We have no sure evidence of its existence before AD 200, but the Jesus Seminar assumes not just that it is as old as our four gospels, but in fact that (in an early form) it is one of the sources of them. This is a remarkable assumption and highly unlikely.

And fourthly, as Richard Hays and Ben Witherington have put it, the Jesus Seminar turns Jesus into 'a talking head'. It ignores the fact that the context in which something is said radically affects the meaning. Our gospels supply a 'narrative context' for Jesus' sayings; in other words, they set them within stories which shape their meaning. Without such a context, sayings become vague and unfocused. For instance, the only full 'red-letter' saying in Mark, according the Jesus Seminar, is 12:17: 'Give to Caesar the things that are Caesar's, and to God the things that are God's' (their translation). But, separated from the hostile question about paying tax (12:14), what does this saying mean? It becomes a portentous utterance worthy of the ancient oracle at Delphi in Greece, which used to issue grand-sounding but meaningless replies to enquirers.

Our gospel writers were well aware of the importance of the *story* of Jesus' ministry within which his teaching was given. To separate off his sayings from the broad enquiry about the background and reliability of all the gospel traditions is like trying to understand tropical butterflies without understanding tropical rainforests, or like studying Lincoln's Gettysburg speech while refusing to discover anything about Lincoln himself.

                                    . . . and more generally

There are good reasons for trusting the gospels! This is how we can reply to the four-point challenge given above.

First, the point about interpretation. We saw in chapter 4 how it is absolutely inevitable that historians will also interpret what they record, and that they will write in order to meet present needs. It is quite true that each gospel writer had distinct emphases and interests, and it is quite probable that these interests were related to the situation of the Christians for whom each was writing. But this is not a valid reason for questioning historical reliability, if every historian does it. We have to decide on other grounds whether the picture presented is reliable or not.

It is certainly possible to distort history by forcing it through the grid of a false interpretation. Modern historians can do it as easily as anyone else. If a scholar says, 'I exclude on principle all stories involving the miraculous', many Christians will argue that this is to base conclusions not on evidence, but on presupposition. But we must be honest. Could the gospel writers also have pushed the story of Jesus through a false grid? In particular, did the facts take second place to their desire to preach, so that the gospels are really just sermons in story form? Or can we be convinced that they really do what Luke claimed and present us with the 'truth' of Jesus? No proof is possible in an area like this, but there are indications which support the gospels' reliability.

Secondly, was Luke alone in having a strong view of the need for accuracy in transmitting the stories of Jesus? At many points, in Acts, his detailed accuracy has been confirmed by archaeology. For instance, he shows extraordinary accuracy in the touchy matter of giving officials their correct titles. In his account of the riot in Ephesus in Acts 19, he give three different kinds of official their correct titles, all rather unusual but all found in inscriptions at Ephesus: 'officials of the province' (Asiarchs) in 19:31; 'the city clerk' in 19:35; and 'proconsuls' in 19:38. Luke uses other technical expressions which have also been found on inscriptions in Ephesus: 'legal assembly' in 19:39; and 'guardian' in 19:35. In his account of Paul's ministry in Thessalonica, Luke twice calls the city officials 'politarchs', an expression unknown in the rest of Greek literature – until it was discovered on inscriptions from Thessalonica. They had adopted a unique name for themselves, which Luke carefully preserves (Acts 17:6, 8). Similarly, he uses several technical expressions to do with the rigging of ships and nautical equipment when he describes the storm and shipwreck in Acts 27, and these have all turned out to be spot-on accurate.

If he was so careful in Acts, may we not presume that he treated the stories of Jesus in the same way? Professor F. F. Bruce remarks that 'Luke's accuracy betokens not only contemporary knowledge but a natural accuracy of mind, and if his trust-worthiness is vindicated in points where he can be checked, we should not assume that he is less trustworthy where we cannot tests his accuracy'.

We may surely presume that Luke is not alone in this. In his preface he refers to 'those who from the first became eye-witnesses and servants of the word', and we must ask who these people were. This could just be Luke's own description of those who 'handed down to us' the gospel stories. But it could also describe a group or class of people recognized by the church at large – people who were able to guarantee the accuracy of their traditions because they had been 'eye-witnesses'. Calling them also 'servants of the word' suggests that they had a kind of semi-official status.

Did the early Christians confuse the words of prophets with the teachings of Jesus? There is no evidence that they did. In 1 Corinthians 7:10–12, 25, 40, Paul carefully distinguishes between the teaching of 'the Lord' and his own teaching, although he regarded himself as a prophet through whom Christ speaks to the church (2 Cor. 13:3). There may have been others who failed to make this distinction, but undoubtedly they would not have got away with it for long!

Thirdly, what about John? His gospel is certainly highly creative in its presentation of Jesus. But is it also inventive? In his case, too, there are some fascinating instances of confirmation at points where he had been suspected of in-accuracy or invention. For instance, the incidental details in the story of the woman at the well (Jn. 4) have an impressive exactness. Jacob's well really is near Sychar (= Shechem, Jn. 4:5–6), a town which was destroyed in AD 67 and therefore was probably in ruins long before John wrote. But he knew it was still standing when Jesus travelled that way. And from Jacob's well, 'this mountain' is visible (4:20) – that is, Mount Gerizim, the sacred mountain of the Samaritans, where 'our fathers worshipped', as the woman says.

Similarly, for many years the pool of Bethesda, to which John refers in 5:2, was not known in any other source, and some scholars suggested that it did not exist. One even suggested that John had given it five 'colonnades' to symbolize the five books of the law, which cannot save. Even the earliest scribes who copied John's gospel had clearly not heard of it, for they were puzzled by the name and suggested variations for it. But then archaeologists found it, in exactly the right place (near the Sheep Gate), with its five colonnades, one on each side and one across the centre. To cap this confirmation of John, one of the Dead Sea Scrolls, published in 1962, contains a reference to it.

John is full of incidental details. For instance, he loves including numbers (see 1:39; 2:6, 20; 4:6; 40; 5:5; 19:14, 39; 21:11) and other tiny details too (*e.g.* 2:12; 6:10, 22–23; 12:3; 18:10). Some have suggested that these are an attempt at 'verisimil-itude'; that is, they are added just to give an 'air' of real history. But this is a very cynical comment. It means that John did not care about detailed historical accuracy himself, but he knew that his readers did, so he put in details to make them think that he cared, too. This would surely not be possible for someone joyfully announcing the coming of truth into the world (Jn. 1:14; 8:32; 14:6; 18:37)!

There is a theological foundation under this emphasis on history. The Word has become flesh (1:14)! What the Word said and did, therefore, matters greatly to John. 'We have seen his glory . . .'; his whole gospel has the quality of testimony to experience. When it comes to Jesus' great 'discourses' in John, therefore, it is highly unlikely that John has written up his favourite sermons and included them. They must be an attempt to represent to his readers the testimony of the incarnate Word. The fact that they are in 'Johannine' style is of no significance, since Jesus taught in Aramaic and the style of the translation has to be the style of the translator.

Having said this, however, it may well be that John has sought to bring out the meaning of the events and sayings he records more explicitly than the other gospels. In Matthew, Mark and Luke, Jesus is reticent in speaking about himself, and in his public teaching he tends to focus on 'the kingdom of God'. In John, on the other hand, he has no hesitation in speaking about himself, and indeed he himself is the usual subject of his discourses. But scholars have long recognized that there is no difference of substance between John and the others here. For all four, Jesus is the vital centre of God's Plan of salvation. John has merely made this clearer in the way he has reported Jesus' proclamation; and so he has sharpened up the issues at stake in our response to him, too.

In the long run, it is a matter of faith whether we accept that the gospel writers, with their highly interpreted picture of Jesus, have actually introduced us to the real Jesus. We can observe that their interpretation of him did not involve them in deliberate fabrication and that they had a deep concern to present the facts as they really were. But they make no bones about their standpoint: Jesus is the Son of God and no-one will truly understand his history without that conviction. So the gospels present us with a take-it-or-leave-it package. If we take it, we must also take great care not to bypass their interpretation but to enter into the marrow of the story as they tell it. An exciting challenge!

Handling the gospels today

We shall end this chapter with some principles of interpretation appropriate for the gospels.

1. Be aware of their social setting and background

Both Jesus and the first Christians, like us, lived in a particular social environment, and much light can be shed on the gospels by discovering what it was like to live in Palestine at that time. In different ways the social, economic, religious and political facts of life in first-century Palestine, or even just in Galilee, have a tremendous impact on our understanding of the gospels. Knowledge of this kind of background is more important for the gospels than for any other part of the Bible, I believe.

Much helpful research has been done on this in recent years, and in fact has served to confirm the reliability of the gospels, because again it has become clear how realistic is their portrait. Much to be recommended is a little book by an eminent German New Testament professor, Gerd Theissen, who has distilled his researches into a novel (*The Shadow of the Galilean*, SCM, 1987). His imaginary character, Andreas, lives in Palestine at the time of Jesus and gets into trouble with many of the people and groups Jesus also rubbed up against. Andreas never actually meets Jesus, but hears much about him. Gerd Theissen tries to convey what it felt like to live in Palestine at that time.

For example, it is important to bear in mind that the country in which Jesus worked was under enemy occupation. The Roman power was enforced by garrisons at strategic places, and ordinary people felt their pressure in the taxes the Romans demanded. The Zealots exerted an opposite pressure on people, trying to get them not to pay. This clearly forms the background to the hot question put to Jesus in Matthew 22:17, and also to

Jesus' command to love our enemies (Mt. 5:44). In the social setting of Palestine at that time, this command was explosive.

Similarly, it will be a great help to discover something about the religious scene in Jesus' day, as part of the setting in which he ministered. Who were the Pharisees and Sadducees, and what did they believe? What did ordinary people believe, and how did they practise their religion? What went on in the temple? Answering questions like these can help us to understand Jesus, and people's reactions to him.

There are many books that can help here. In addition to Bible dictionaries and introductions to the gospels, one scholarly book that is packed with information and is also highly readable is by Ben Witherington III, *The Jesus Quest: The Third Search for the Jew of Nazareth* (Paternoster, 1995). The Crossway Bible Guides on the gospels fill out the background where appropriate: for instance, David Hewitt's Guide to Mark has information boxes on (among other things) synagogue worship, leprosy, tax collectors, Sabbath observance, demon possession, Herod, and scribal traditions.

2. See the gospels as wholes

Only when we read the gospels as dramas, complete in themselves, can we really respect them for what they are. We need to explore the order of their material, for it is this which consciously distinguished the gospels from what preceded them. Unfortunately, this is not how we usually read them. Bible-reading schemes tend, inevitably, to divide the gospels up into their individual stories and sections and thus to isolate them from each other again. But this is precisely what the gospel writers were seeking to remedy! They could have issued anthologies of stories and sayings, perhaps classified under subjects. But in all likelihood this had been done already. They wanted to attempt something greater: a presentation of Jesus that led the reader to understanding, not just to knowledge, by putting each individual story and saying in a context that enabled right interpretation of it. To do this they linked related stories and sayings together by themes, although these stories had previously circulated singly, or differently connected to each other. So we need to ask of each incident or saying: how does this fit into the message and 'story' of the whole gospel?

For instance, there are many stories that illustrate the conflict between Jesus and the religious authorities. Read individually, that is all they do. One such story is the healing of the paralytic, in Mark 2:1–12, which contains the scribes' sharp reaction, 'Why does this fellow talk like that? He's blaspheming!' The story could be read in isolation, but, when we read it as part of Mark's gospel, it takes on new significance. We realize that Mark has made it the first in a string of stories all touching on the conflict between Jesus and the religious authorities. The series reaches a climax in Mark 3:6, following the healing of the man with the withered hand; 'the Pharisees went out and began to plot with the Herodians how they might kill Jesus'.

Rabbis often disagreed with each other, so conflict was not necessarily life-threatening! But Mark shows that, in Jesus' case, it was. Already the cross is being foreshadowed. Having noticed this, we go back to Mark 1:22 and read it in a new way: 'The people were amazed at his teaching, because he taught them as one who had authority, not as the teachers of the law.' The final throwaway phrase here has much more significance than it seems when we first meet it. Not only is it preparing us, within a few verses of the start of the gospel, for the clash that will lead to Jesus' execution, it is also showing us in advance how to interpret that clash when we meet it later: it is a conflict of authority. Jesus exercises an authority that sets him apart from all other teachers and even, to some extent, from the law.

This 'reading as a whole' is vital. Let us take another example, this time from the book of Acts. At first sight Acts look rather jumbled, with one episode just following on from another until it ends abruptly with Paul under house arrest in Rome (Acts 28:30–31). Some scholars, puzzled by the ending, have suggested that Luke intended to write more but was prevented from doing so. Yet when we look more closely, we begin to see a theme that holds the book together and gives it its 'message'. At the start of the book, Luke records Jesus' commission to the disciples:

> You will receive power when the Holy Spirit comes on you; and you will be my witnesses in Jerusalem, and in all Judea and Samaria, and to the ends of the earth. *(Acts 1:8)*

The story then follows this geographical pattern, starting in Jerusalem (1:12 – 7:60). The Jerusalem section ends with the stoning of Stephen, which deliberately looks back to and matches the crucifixion of Jesus. The Jerusalem authorities seal their rejection of Jesus by their rejection of his representative and the gospel he preached, and so the gospel is sent to others. The story moves out into Judea and Samaria (see 8:1), and in 9:31 Luke summarizes the story so far:

> Then the church throughout Judea, Galilee and Samaria enjoyed a time of peace. It was strengthened; and encouraged by the Holy Spirit, it grew in numbers.

Then Luke introduces the next great outward movement, starting with the story of Peter's visit to Joppa (9:32–43). Little did Peter realize that in Joppa he would receive the vision that would herald the expansion of the church into the Gentile world (Acts 10). Luke follows the exciting story of that expansion, focusing on the ministry of Paul from chapter 13 onwards. Rome looms from 19:21 onwards, where Paul first makes plans to go there. The last ten chapters of Acts tell the extended story of his journey to Rome, fraught with difficulties but ultimately triumphant, just as Luke framed the second half of his gospel around Jesus' journey to Jerusalem. That, too, ended in what looked like defeat but was not. Similarly, Paul's arrival in chains in Rome tells us that the preaching of the gospel will triumph. The Plan set out in 1:8 will be fulfilled, although the church must expect to bear the likeness of her

Lord, appearing defeated, but actually victorious.

Undoubtedly all the apostles were active in spreading the gospel, and the church was expanding in many directions. Historians may object to Luke's selectivity, but he focuses on Paul because he wants to convey this particular message, which will be true for the church in every age, not just in the first century.

3. Watch for recurrent themes and ideas

It is thrilling to spot the distinct themes and interests of each gospel and to note how they are developed. The gospels are like the Old Testament histories in this respect. They leave us, the readers, to make intelligent connections between passages which are linked by theme – sometimes very subtly.

For instance, the themes of blindness and seeing are important to Mark. The quotation of Isaiah 6:9 in Mark 4:12 introduces us to the idea of people seeing but not perceiving. We have already met several people in this category in his gospel, and the parable of the sower (in which the quotation comes) illustrates the variety of response to Jesus. Some people see clearly and respond gladly; others do not see at all and reject him; and there are stages in between. This theme then receives a special development in chapter 8. Here we meet the Pharisees again (8:11–13); they see Jesus feed the four thousand and still ask for a 'sign'!

Then we discover that Jesus is worried about the disciples: where do they come on this scale of spiritual perception (see 8:14–21)? Next, Jesus performs a two-stage restoration of sight on a blind man (8:22–26): first he receives the ability to see (24), then the power to perceive, to make sense of what he sees (25). The following episode is Peter's confession of Christ at Caesarea Philippi. He too has had perception added to sight, on a spiritual level. In its context, the story of the healing of the blind man in Mark 8:22–26 acts as a powerful parable of what must happen spiritually as well.

Luke has many special interests and themes. They include the

Holy Spirit; salvation; prayer; Jesus' ministry to the outcasts of society and those whom others pass by (Samaritans, lepers, shepherds, Gentiles); women; judgment on Israel and the restoration of Israel; the relationship with secular authorities, particualrly the Romans; and the fulfilment of prophecy. All these themes are well worth following through both his gospel and Acts.

John's gospel is built around a network of interlocking themes of this type; they are the key to the study of John. Many of his vital themes are introduced in his prologue (1:1–18), where he gives us a kind of checklist to keep in mind as we read. But there are many other themes that appear as the gospel develops.

One particularly interesting and important theme is that of the Jewish festivals. John shows Jesus' involvement with each of them in turn: Passover (chapter 6), Tabernacles (chapters 7 – 9), and Dedication (chapter 10). In each case the theology of the festival concerned – its meaning for the participants and its Old Testament background – is brought into the discussion and the teaching Jesus gives. For instance, in chapter 6, the Passover chapter, Jesus presents himself as the one sent by God to bring about a new exodus, greater than the exodus the crowd were going to Jerusalem to celebrate. He is seen to be the 'second Moses' who feeds the people miraculously in the desert, and claims to be in person 'the bread of life'.

John expects his readers to know what went on at these festivals. He does not tell us, for instance, that there were special water and light ceremonies at the Feast of Tabernacles. He simply reports Jesus' claim, at the feast, to be the source of living water (7:37–39) and to be the light of the world (8:12).

Water is a good example of a smaller theme in John, which links together important ideas under its common image. It appears for the first time in 1:26 with the mention of John's baptism 'in water'. Then it reappears in 2:1–11, where Jesus changes water into wine, picturing the transformation of Judaism (the water was there for rites of purification, 2:6). Water becomes linked with the Holy Spirit in 3:5, and this link then remains through its further development: the vital further references are 3:23–26; 4:10–14; 5:7–8; 6:35; 7:37–39; 13:5–12 and 19:34–35. John builds on Isaiah's use of water imagery:

> For I will pour water on the thirsty land,
>   and streams on the dry ground;
> I will pour out my Spirit on your offspring,
>   and my blessing on your descendants.
>
> *(Is. 44:3)*

Thus he associates water with the Holy Spirit and with the transformation and new birth of God's people.

4. Watch out for individuals

The Old Testament histories show an interest in people, and this interest continues in the New. We meet many minor characters in the gospels and Acts, and they all repay careful study. Often, they are used to illustrate points made elsewhere in the story. Zacchaeus, for example, illustrates two ideas dear to Luke: Jesus' concern for society's rejects, and God's faithfulness to his promises to Abraham (Lk. 19:1–10). Mark presents a very 'human' picture of Jesus' disciples. We see them warts and all, and so are able to sympathize with them as they struggle to understand who Jesus is.

In addition to the main actors in the drama, Acts has a large supporting cast. Again we realize how important individual discipleship is to God as we read of people like Stephen, Philip, Aeneas, Dorcas, Cornelius, Barnabas, Timothy, Lydia, Silas, Apollos, Aquilla and Priscilla. Some of the characters are finely drawn, like generous and big-minded Barnabas. Luke draws an attractive picture of him. He was able to see the grace of God where others could not see it, both in individuals and in the expansion of the church among the Gentiles (Acts 4:36–37; 11:22–26; 13:1–3; 15:35–41).

John, too, mentions many individuals and manages to

convey vivid pictures of them in just a few words. The references to Nicodemus, for example, clearly show him as someone deeply attracted to Jesus but who simply could not face the risk of jeopardizing his position as a member of the Sanhedrin by becoming an open disciple (Jn. 3:1–2; 7:50–51; 19:39; see also 12:42–43). In a different way the man healed of blindness in John 9 comes across so clearly in his 'cussedness': he will not be browbeaten, but will tell the truth as he sees it, whatever people may say!

People used to carry portraits of their loved ones in tiny lockets around their necks. Tremendous skills were necessary to produce those minute portraits. They were so tiny that many details just could not be reproduced, yet they had to convey an exact impression of the face. The gospels are like this. In comparison with other biographies they are minute, and yet Christian faith confesses that their portrait of Jesus is 'the real thing'. This was clearly the feeling at the time, as the gospels became the standard resource of the church, and the earlier collections and accounts dropped into disuse.

And their size is a blessing in itself. Like a locket around the neck, we can keep peeping into them and feasting our eyes on the Saviour we love. And the more we look, the more we shall get to know him. We need to soak ourselves in the gospels more than in any other part of the Bible, simply because of the subject. Here we meet Jesus face to face and so here our faith has its roots and its foundation.

'Thus says the Lord!'

Handling biblical prophecy

Joel Green begins his excellent book *How To Read Prophecy* (IVP, 1984) with a story that will ring bells with many. An excited friend burst into his room one day with the announcement, 'Jesus is coming back, Joel – before Saturday!' His friend had listened to a tape which taught it all so clearly and scripturally and left no room for doubt. The second coming had to take place that week! Sceptical, Joel Green agreed to listen to the tape – on the following Sunday!

Even though he was sceptical at the time, he is also honest about the way in which such claims attracted and gripped him as a young Christian. He is not alone in this. Does the Bible really open the future to us in this kind of detail? We can't help being drawn to the thought that it does. There have been many who have made this claim, both within the church and on its fringes. The writings of Hal Lindsey have been bestsellers, with their claim to be able to relate recent events directly to biblical prophecies. My copy of his book *The Late Great Planet Earth* (fifth impression, 1974), proclaims on the cover, 'Over 1,600,000 copies in print.' This speaks for itself about the compelling power of such interpretations of biblical prophecy. And of course the Jehovah's Witnesses build their whole system on the view that we are in the last few days now, with the battle of

Armageddon (Rev. 16:16) just around the corner. This kind of interpretation makes the Bible seem so right and so relevant to life today, prophesying about the events through which we are living.

But is this the right approach?

What is prophecy?

We are happy to call the whole Bible 'inspired' and to think of it as a 'revelation' from God and of God. So it comes as a shock to learn that the various books of the Bible differ from each other quite markedly when it comes to what they actually claim for themselves.

The histories claim to record past events by which God revealed himself. They set out to tell us of a revelation that took place before they were written. They do not directly claim that they themselves are similarly 'revelation' – although we believe they are, precisely because they record and interpret God's action in the world. Other books, like the Psalms and the wisdom books, do not claim to be a revelation of God at all. They are responses to revelation, in their own eyes (though here, too, we are happy to claim more for them). But there is a further class of books which claim to be revelation in themselves, and not just to record it or to respond to it. These are the books to which we give the name 'prophetic' because they claim to contain the direct words of God in human speech: 'Thus says the LORD . . .'

Actually, we need to be a little more careful about the title 'prophetic'. Thought of in this way, the letters of Paul would have to be classified as prophecy (see 2 Cor. 13:3), and Jesus himself clearly exercised a 'prophetic' ministry. But we do not usually call either Paul's letters or the gospels 'prophecy', because we reserve this title for a certain type of literature, as well as using it to describe a distinct style of revelation. By 'the prophets', we mean the prophetic books of the Old Testament, lumping together the massive books of Isaiah, Jeremiah and

Ezekiel with the thirteen so-called 'minor prophets' (Daniel to Malachi). We do not normally include any New Testament books in this category, although Revelation calls itself a prophecy (Rev. 1:3) and Paul's letters clearly fit the bill. Even though it is rather arbitrary to separate them, we are dealing with Paul and Revelation in other chapters and focusing in this chapter chiefly on the books normally labelled 'prophetic'.

Here is a possible definition of biblical prophecy: it is *the communication, through an appointed human messenger, of a directed, immediate word of God, with local and universal significance*. It is 'directed' because prophecy is never general and timeless, but always speaks to a specific human situation. It is 'immediate' because, although a human messenger is used, God himself speaks. This claim is made without hesitation by the biblical prophets. They have tremendous confidence in their own reliability as God's spokesmen. Throughout their writings there is no qualification of their ringing 'Thus says the LORD!' This confidence stems from their awareness of being appointed by God, which means being allowed to join his 'council' and hear his plans. Amos opens a window on to the prophet's inner life when he writes, 'Surely the Sovereign LORD does nothing without revealing his plan to his servants the prophets' (Am. 3:7). To be an Old Testament prophet was a privilege indeed.

This is why I added 'with universal significance' to the definition above. God's word through the prophets is always concerned with a specific, local problem or need, but from the start it was never limited to its local setting. The very fact that the prophets' oracles were collected into books showed a demand for their wider circulation. A process of interpretation and reapplication began straight away. And this process carried right on into the New Testament, where the words of the prophets were applied to Jesus and a new stage of interpretation began. As we think about how we should handle the prophets today, we need to look carefully at the way they are handled in the New Testament.

What were the prophets doing?

Three things distinguish the writings of the prophets from other biblical writings.

First, the prophets always ministered in a crisis. They were God's means of interpreting a crisis in Israel's life: warning the people, accusing them or giving them hope, whatever was appropriate at the time.

Secondly, the prophets used language in a special way. Very often, their oracles are actually poems, using much imagery as well as special poetic styles. This makes translation and interpretation especially difficult. 'Apocalyptic' is the name given to the special style of prophetic writing we find particularly in Daniel and Revelation, where vivid images are crowded on top of each other. But all prophetic writing is distinguished by such symbolic language.

Thirdly, prophetic writing is distinguished by a sense of the pressure of the future on the present. The prophets were by no means always predicting the future. According to Joel Green, less than 1% of Old Testament prophecy is concerned with prediction. But they were always borne along by a sense of urgency, because they saw the world from God's perspective, and the future realities of judgment and restoration danced vividly before their minds. The burden of their message was questions like: 'Can't you see where you're heading? Don't you know who God is? Won't you respond to his word before it's too late? Haven't you grasped what his Plan is for you and the world?'

Handling prophecy today

We shall look more closely at each of these three vital features of prophecy and turn them into principles of interpretation.

1. Be aware of the crisis

It is important that we know the context into which the prophets wrote, or their precise message will escape us. For instance, Isaiah's famous 'Immanuel' prophecy (Is. 7:14) was given in a very particular situation, and knowledge of it is essential if we are to grasp the true wonder of 'God with us'. The promise of the Immanuel-child appears in the middle of a prophecy of judgment on God's people. Faced with an imminent invasion, King Ahaz has just refused to put his trust in the Lord and, instead, is depending on his own resources (Is. 7:1–12). Isaiah then unfolds, with horrifying clarity, the judgment to come. The Lord will indeed deliver Judah from this immediate threat, but only because the invaders will themselves be swallowed up by a huge force sweeping right across the whole region – and swamping Judah along with her enemies. The massive army of Assyria is coming (Is. 7:13–25)!

In the middle of this prophecy, the promise of the birth of the Immanuel-child is given. Summing it up in the next chapter, Isaiah compares this Assyrian army to the sudden surge of water in a river after a storm. It will

> sweep on into Judah, swirling over it,
>> passing through it and reaching up to the neck.
> Its outstretched wings will cover the breadth of your land,
>> O Immanuel!

(Is. 8:8)

The reappearance of 'Immanuel' here is so striking. The problem is that God is about to act in judgment on Judah. But Judah is called Immanuel's land. So the Immanuel promise is not just a general one, that God will be with his people, but more precisely that even when he judges them, he will not desert them but will work for their salvation.

Examples of the crises that underlie prophetic ministry could be multiplied. Elijah ministered in a crisis of faithfulness under King Ahab (1 Ki. 17 – 21). Amos faced a crisis of morals in affluence, under the mighty King Jeroboam II. Jeremiah exercised a long ministry all through the last years of Judah and the eventual destruction of Jerusalem, and on into the time of the exile. Ezekiel ministered in Babylon to those in exile. Joel's prophecy is hard to date, but the crisis is precise: the people are trying to come to terms with the devastation caused by a massive swarm of locusts. In the New Testament, the book of Revelation ministers to seven small congregations facing hostility and persecution and trying to come to terms with their own weakness. Paul's letters are all called into being by a crisis of some kind, and the meaning of what he writes is bound up with the nature of the crisis in each case.

We need to understand these situations or we shall miss the meaning.

2. Know how to handle the language

The prophetic writings of the Bible use language in special ways, and this sets us three particular challenges.

First, we must be sensitive to biblical symbolism. The prophets use much symbolism and figurative language. This causes us difficulties because figurative language depends on our being able to spot the correspondence between the symbol and the thing symbolized. The problem is, symbols are often closely tied to the culture of Bible times. For instance, wadis are a geographical feature typical of hot climates, so interpreters who live in temperate areas of the world have not had the experience which underlies Isaiah's picture of seeing water suddenly appear from nowhere in a dry river bed, and swell to a raging torrent within minutes (Is. 8:8).

We can illustrate the challenge further from the same passage (Is. 8:6–8). Isaiah contrasts this torrent (which symbolizes the invading Assyrian army) with 'the gentle flowing waters of Shiloah' that the people have rejected. Unpacking this further image shows how in fact there are two distinct problems in handling language of this sort. I can go to Otto Kaiser's commentary on Isaiah (SCM, 1972) and discover that Shiloah was 'a channel with a very slight fall which led the water from the spring of Gihon along the edge of the eastern hill of the city' (Jerusalem). But getting this information is just the first step. I then have to decide what Isaiah intends the stream to symbolize in the context of his prophecy here.

Contrasted with a mighty torrent of judgment from abroad, this quiet stream, gently providing the daily needs of Jerusalem, could symbolize the Lord's gracious and constant sustenance of his people. Ahaz has rejected the Lord's promise to go on looking after them. But perhaps there is more to it. Ahaz was out inspecting Jerusalem's water supply when Isaiah met him and challenged him to put his trust in the Lord, not in human resources (Is. 7:3). With this in the background, Isaiah's image in 8:6 takes on new force. The very thing in which Ahaz wanted to place his confidence (Jerusalem's water supply, which would enable the city to survive a siege) will prove his undoing as the gentle stream turns into a dreadful flood of judgment. The gentle stream came from the Lord anyway: why could Ahaz not trust the Lord to keep the promise implicit in that constant supply?

This is the beauty of symbolic language: it can say something very subtle in a wonderfully compelling way. Its meaning appears as we reflect carefully on its cultural background, and on its literary and biblical setting.

As a further example, we shall look at a difficult verse in Peter's sermon on the day of Pentecost. He quotes from Joel, saying that Joel's prophecy has been fulfilled in the outpouring of the Holy Spirit, and includes the verse,

The sun will be turned to darkness
  and the moon to blood
  before the coming of the great and glorious day of the Lord.

(Acts 2:20)

How should we interpret such 'astronomical' symbolism? We meet symbols like these throughout the prophetic books, and particularly in apocalyptic literature (*e.g.* Rev. 6:12–14; 8:12). This example can give us principles to apply whenever we meet language of this kind.

It is clearly not meant literally, either in Joel or in Acts. Literally, it is a description of a double eclipse, of both sun and moon. But this did not take place on the day of Pentecost, even though Peter claimed that the prophecy was fulfilled that day. The eclipse language is symbolic of something else. But of what?

Eclipses and other astronomical events were often regarded as 'portents' in the ancient world – that is, as signs that significant events were happening or were about to happen. It is interesting that biblical symbols are sometimes drawn from a pagan reservoir. Perhaps, both for Joel and for Peter, this language symbolized simply an earth-shattering moment in God's calendar. Viewed as an event in world history, it was a tiny happening in a remote corner of the Roman empire; but viewed in the light of the Plan, the gift of the Spirit at Pentecost shakes the foundations. It is a creation event, anticipating 'the day of the Lord'.

But could it be more than this? Within the context of the Bible, the darkening of the sun and turning of things into blood remind us not of an eclipse, but of the plagues inflicted as judgment on the Egyptians, just before the exodus (see Ex. 7:14–24; 10:21–29). And the 'day of the Lord' in the Bible is usually the moment of judgment. So is this the force of these symbols too? Perhaps we are being shown that the gift of the Spirit to this international crowd, anticipating the worldwide church, is an implicit judgment on the nation that crucified Jesus. One of the 'signs' in the previous verse is smoke, which likewise is a symbol of judgment throughout the Bible. Peter goes on to talk about his hearers' responsibility for crucifying Jesus (Acts 2:23, 36).

We could go even further. If the signs accompanying the gift of the Holy Spirit remind us of the events that led up to the exodus, what of Pentecost itself? Are we being prompted to think of it as a new exodus? God is stepping in to deliver his people, not now from political bondage, but from spiritual. There are other hints that this may be in mind. For instance, in the next chapter, Peter deliberately compares Jesus to Moses (Acts 3:22–23). All these people have been brought out of their many countries of origin (Acts 2:9–11), in order to form the nucleus of a new people of God, indwelt by his Spirit.

How can we be sure that we are not reading all this into the symbols in Acts 2:20, rather than drawing out their true force? We can't. But we are looking in the right places and reading in the right way. Such symbols draw meaning from their associations, which can be many and various. An idea of the general background of the writer's culture gives us our first clues, and then by turning to previous uses of the same images in the Bible we can fill out the likely associations that were in the writer's mind. All the time, as we try out different ideas, we look for other indications in the context that we are on the right lines.

Secondly, we must be aware of the importance of prophetic 'signs'. 'Signs' played a big role in prophetic ministry in several ways. We need to grasp what they were and how they functioned. Sometimes prophets were called upon actually to perform signs, which are like extensions of the symbolic language we have just been considering. They are acted words, messages turned into a striking action which does not just illustrate the message, but makes it very definite, conveying a special determination of God to carry out what he says he will do.

The Bible is full of examples of such signs, which are a little strange to us today. Agabus took Paul's belt and tied up his own hands and feet with it, before delivering the word, 'The Holy Spirit says, "In this way the Jews of Jerusalem will bind the owner of this belt and will hand him over to the Gentiles"' (Acts 21:11). The action was an advance performance of the deed itself, making it absolutely certain that it would take place.

Even more vividly, Ahijah the Shilonite took off his cloak in front of Jeroboam, tore it into twelve pieces and gave ten of them to Jeroboam with the word from the Lord, 'See, I am going to tear the kingdom out of Solomon's hand and give you ten tribes' (1 Ki. 11:31). According to the story, it had not occurred to Jeroboam to rebel against Solomon, but once this very public 'acted oracle' had taken place and Solomon heard about it, Jeroboam had to flee the kingdom and wait for God's moment of fulfilment.

Sometimes the prophet becomes a sign in his own person. Isaiah had to walk around naked and barefoot for three years, to symbolize the imminent downfall of Egypt (Is. 20:3). Ezekiel had to lie on his left side in front of a picture of Jerusalem under siege for 390 days (Ezk. 4), and then had to shave off his hair and beard and do symbolic things to it (Ezk. 5). Hosea had to marry a prostitute and then later buy her back from her life of adultery, symbolizing the relationship between the Lord and Israel (Ho. 1:2; 3:1–5); and both he and Isaiah had to give their children extraordinary names, making them walking signs to all they met (Ho. 1:4ff.; 2:21ff.; Is. 7:3; 8:1–4).

Old Testament prophetic signs like these are the background to the miracles of Jesus. His miracles were more than just individual acts of mercy to people in need; they were 'words' to accompany his teaching, 'acted oracles' which make the reality of the kingdom of God clear: 'if I drive out demons by the finger of God, then the kingdom of God has come to you!' (Lk. 11:20).

But the prophets were not just appointed to do significant things. They were, more importantly, called to declare the significance of the situations facing God's people, or of the great events they were caught up in. The whole burden of Ezekiel's ministry was to explain the reasons for the destruction of Jerusalem and the exile of God's people in Babylon. What did these events mean? How could they be fitted into God's Plan? Jeremiah had to exercise a similar ministry before the exile took place, explaining why it would happen and how and when it would end. Joel tried to help people understand why God had allowed a calamitous locust swarm, and he turned it into a picture of the Day of the Lord. Daniel explained the meaning of dreams and visions, and was called upon to give insight into the rise and fall of empires over the centuries leading up to the establishment of God's kingdom over all the earth.

This is where prediction fits in. Sometimes the prophets were enabled to announce events in advance, so that when they took place, people would know how to interpret and respond to them. The clearest example of this is Isaiah. As the book stands, he faces the inevitability of judgment on Israel, and exile; but then he looks beyond it to eventual restoration, even giving the name of the Persian king through whom the political restoration of Israel will take place (Is. 44:28; 45:1, 13), some 150 years ahead of time. Some scholars do not accept that this is prophecy, and regard the section of the book that speaks of the restoration from exile as contemporary with the event – even though the fact that it was predicted in advance is used as an argument in the book itself (Is. 42:9; 44–7).

Moving over into the New Testament, we find that Paul's ministry is similarly rooted in real life, and focuses on the prophetic explanation of the facts. Many early Jewish Christians found the indiscriminate gift of the Holy Spirit to the Gentiles hard to understand in the light of the Plan, and the books of Romans and Galatians are largely devoted to explaining what God is up to, and what this inclusion of the Gentiles signifies.

Thirdly, we *must not be carried away by the literalist argument*. This is a vital principle to remember when handling prophetic language. Evangelical Christians who want to be serious about the authority of the Bible are attracted by the view that, as John F. Walvoord puts it, 'Scripture should be interpreted in its normative, literal sense, except in such instances where a figurative or nonliteral interpretation is obviously indicated'.

Great care needs to be taken about this. With prophetic language it is actually more appropriate to allow full scope for the use of symbolism and 'nonliteral' expressions than to seek to minimize them. In any case, this view does not take seriously the way things become symbols within the Bible itself.

The temple is a good example of this. Of course, it was a

literal building, erected by Solomon as a permanent successor to the tabernacle. But even as a literal building, it stood for something else: the presence of the Lord in the midst of his people, his commitment to them, and his provision of the means of forgiveness. Ezekiel was carried off into exile ten years before Jerusalem and the temple were destroyed by the Babylonians, but he knew that these events would follow. In particular, he was shown in a vision the departure of the glory of the Lord from the temple, because of the awful sin found there (Ezk. 10). That was the vital event, not the demolishing of the bricks and mortar six years later.

But Ezekiel knew that this was not the end of the Lord's commitment to his people. He passed on a message from God: 'Although I sent them far away among the nations . . . yet for a little while I have been a sanctuary for them in the countries where they have gone' (Ezk. 11:16). The Lord has been all that the temple meant, without the physical building. This is the meaning of the amazing vision of God's glory among the exiles, by the River Kebar in Babylon (1:1) – not in the temple in Jerusalem. So we are already prepared for the departure of God's glory from the temple (Ezk. 10:4).

Ezekiel develops these thoughts. God will one day live again among his people in the land; he will do so by transforming their hearts and rebuilding their inner life (Ezk. 11:17–21). The vision of the Valley of Dry Bones (Ezk. 37:1–14) pictures this inner restoration of the whole nation and its return from exile. But its restoration depends on a new kind of indwelling; not now the glory of God in a physical temple, but his Spirit in the hearts of his people.

So when Ezekiel later prophesies the rebuilding of the temple (chapters 40 – 48), we are already disposed not to interpret it literally. And in fact he could not intend it literally. The measurements he gives for both the temple and the sur-rounding land (chapters 40 – 42, 45) could not be worked out 'on the ground'. In fact, when the Israelites who returned from exile were inspired by the prophet Haggai to rebuild the temple, they did not attempt to follow Ezekiel's pattern. They recognized that his picture was an idealized one in which God dwells in the middle of his people, like the temple at the symmetrical centre of the land.

Ezekiel prepares us for the New Testament, where the temple is treated symbolically again: it is a symbol of the body of Jesus, torn down and rebuilt (Jn. 2:20–21), and then of the church, the company of believers built upon Jesus the cornerstone and indwelt by the Holy Spirit (1 Cor. 3:16; Eph. 2:19–22). The literal temple, torn down in AD 70, has already been rebuilt as the body of Christ.

Within the whole sweep of biblical thought, therefore, it makes no sense to expect a literal fulfilment of the prophecies of rebuilding the temple. The same applies, I believe, to other Old Testament prophecies which are sometimes understood literally. For instance, the New Testament applies the promises of possessing the land of Israel, given literally to Abraham and his descendants, to the *spiritual* possession of God's kingdom. We see this happening very clearly in the letter to the Hebrews: God promised Israel 'rest' in the land, but Israel failed to enter all that the promise meant (Heb. 3:16–19) and so 'Sabbath-rest remains still unclaimed by God's people!' (Heb. 4:9, my translation), to be entered simply through faith in Christ.

The argument is subtle but clear: Israel did, of course, enter the promised land but not the 'rest', that is, the sharing of the life of God himself which was the whole purpose of the promise. The argument of this section of Hebrews (3:7 – 4:11) builds on Psalm 95:7–11, where David invites people to enter God's rest 'today', implying that they had not entered it simply by dwelling in the promised land. Only in Christ does this spiritual dimension of the promise find fulfiment, and the physical side of it then slips away (it is 'obsolete and ageing', and 'will soon disappear', Heb. 8:13).

Similarly, we should not interpret literally the prophecies of an idyllic paradise on earth, given for instance by Isaiah: 'The wolf will live with the lamb, the leopard will lie down with the goat . . .' (Is. 11:6). These are very vivid symbols for a restored and harmonious earth from which all sin and hatred have been banished – a vision ultimately to be fulfilled in the new heaven and earth that Isaiah also prophesied (65:17–25), and that will fully replace this present heaven and earth (2 Pet. 3:10–13; Rev. 21:1).

This brings us to the third and final principle of interpreting prophecy.

3. Remember its purpose throughout the Bible

Why did the prophets write? It is most misleading to treat them as spiritual almanacs, writing history in advance of the event. In the next chapter we shall look at 'apocalyptic' writing, especially Daniel and Revelation, where this view is especially influential. Yes, they were deeply concerned with the future; we summarized this concern above by saying that they felt the pressure of the future as they foresaw both judgment and salvation coming in God's Plan. But they wrote about the future in order to change the present. In fact, it is clear that the underlying purpose of their ministry was often to prevent what they foresaw from happening. Their chief desire was to enable people to live better in the present, because of the future.

Jonah is a good example. He knew that God intended the destruction of Nineveh, the capital of the Assyrian empire. He knew, too, that if he obeyed God and went to warn them, they would probably repent and the destruction would be averted. So he ran away – because he wanted to see these enemies of Israel destroyed! He knew full well that God would not have told him to go there had he not intended to bring them to repentance, rather than destruction. Prophets announce coming judgment, but largely so that it may not happen. For they also announce the means of salvation.

Amos did the same thing for Israel, proclaiming coming judgment in horrifying, vivid language. But through it all rings a different note:

> Seek good, not evil,
>   that you may live.
> Then the LORD God Almighty will be with you,
>   just as you say he is.
> Hate evil, love good;
>   maintain justice in the courts.
> Perhaps the LORD God Almighty will have mercy
>   on the remant of Joseph.
>
> *(Am. 5:14–15)*

The presence of this offer gives all the threats a different flavour.

This gives us one of the vital keys for handling the prophets today; for we are in the same situation! We, too, need to shape our lives now to prepare for future judgment. Paul is uncompromising:

> We must all appear before the judgment seat of Christ, that each one may receive what is due to him for the things done while in the body, whether good or bad.   *(2 Cor. 5:10)*

Peter gives it a cosmic dimension:

> The heavens will disappear with a roar . . .
>   Since everything will be destroyed in this way, what kind of people ought you to be? You ought to live holy and godly lives as you look forward to the day of God and speed its coming.   *(2 Pet. 3:10–12)*

All too easily, we Christians lose sight of the day of judgment because we think that the coming of Jesus has changed all that. There is no longer any need to talk about judgment, we feel, because Jesus has brought all that Old Testament doom and gloom to an end. But this is to misunderstand both the prophets and the New Testament. The prophets certainly underlined the horror of sin and the inevitability of judgment, but they never left people without hope. Hope is implicit in their preaching of judgment, for recognizing your problem is essential if you are to find the way out of it.

In fact, this underlies the so-called 'oracles to the nations' which feature prominently in some prophets (see Am. 1:3 – 2:5; Is. 13 – 23; Je. 46 – 51; Ezk. 25 – 32; and the whole book of Nahum is a message to Nineveh). These oracles are largely taken up with announcing the Lord's judgment on these nations, but the very fact that he announces it contains an implicit offer of salvation. The message comes to them from Israel, so that, as in the case of Naaman (2 Ki. 5), the way is open for them to find out more about the Lord and to get right with him.

They announced the coming of the Messiah, who would be God's means of saving people from his own judgment on sin; and we believe Jesus is that Messiah. But the New Testament is very clear: he does not deliver us from *facing* judgment, but from *being condemned* at the judgment (see *e.g.* Rom. 2:10; 8:1; 14:10–12; 1 Cor. 3:10–15; 2 Cor. 5:10; Gal. 6:7–10; Heb. 10:19–25). We are responsible for our lives, and may mess them up. We need to stand beside God's people of the Old Testament, catch from the prophets their vision of the blazing holiness of God, and sense the tremendous urgency in their appeal: 'Rend your heart and not your garments.' 'Return, O Israel, to the LORD your God. Your sins have been your downfall!' 'Prepare to meet your God, O Israel' (Joel 2:13; Ho. 14:1; Am. 4:12).

Looking back through Jesus

Just as the prophets looked ahead to a future in which the Messiah figured largely, so we should look back to them through the Messiah they foretold. We see this happening in the New Testament. We thought above about Peter's quotation of Joel on the day of Pentecost. Something further we could notice is the way he fills out the meaning of Joel, by interpreting it in the light of Jesus. In particular, Joel's meaning in 2:32 (Acts 2:21) has been transformed: 'And everyone who calls on the name of the Lord will be saved.' For Peter, 'calling on the Lord' now means 'believing in Jesus', for 'God has made this Jesus, whom you crucified, both Lord and Christ' (Acts 2:36). Paul adds another dimension when he quotes the same verse in Romans 10:13: he emphasizes the 'everyone', and interprets it as an offer to all people, Gentiles and Jews alike. Joel probably just had Jews in mind; but I am sure that he would not be unhappy with this application of his prophecy, or with Peter's.

This kind of thing happens throughout the New Testament. It is not that the New Testament authors simply impose their own interpretation on the Old Testament. They believe that Jesus is the fulfilment of the Plan (which they too traced through the Old Testament), and therefore that he is the hidden meaning of the Old Testament. Paul puts it in a nutshell in the little 'doxology' with which he finishes Romans:

> Now to him who is able to establish you by my gospel and the proclamation of Jesus Christ, according to the revelation of the mystery hidden for long ages past, but now revealed and made known *through the prophetic writings* by the command of the eternal God, so that all nations might believe and obey him – to the only wise God be glory for ever through Jesus Christ! Amen. *(Rom. 16:25–27)*

For Paul, the 'prophetic writings' make Christ known, because he is the fulfilment of that great Plan which holds the whole Bible together, the Plan to save the world from the rebellion of Eden and its consequences. We may follow his example and let the prophets teach us about Jesus.

Signs in heaven above

Making sense of Daniel and Revelation

The book of Revelation is a great read. I well remember the deep impression it made upon me as a young Christian, when I sat on my bed at college and simply read it right through. There was much of it that I failed to understand, but that didn't seem to matter, because it 'got' to me. I was bowled over by a tremendous sense of the sovereignty and power of God, and of his rule over every part of the world, including the evil in it. I remember trying to convey my excitement over it to my non-Christian neighbour. He seemed to think I had taken leave of my senses.

Perhaps this is the right way to approach it, anyway: not to worry too much about the details of interpretation but simply to absorb it. The 'seven letters' with which it begins all end with the exhortation, 'He who has an ear, let him hear what the Spirit says to the churches' (Rev. 2:7, *etc.*). This reminds us of the way Jesus concludes the parable of the sower: 'He who has ears to hear, let him hear' (Mk. 4:9). Jesus is not implying that some of his hearers have had nasty accidents to their aural orifices. He is aware that, while all will hear him physically, they need to have a capacity for spiritual hearing as well, otherwise the parable of the sower (and all the others) will be no more than pretty stories.

Revelation is rather like Jesus' parables in this respect. A person who has the ability to hear spiritually is able to learn about the kingdom of God from the parables. But very often the detailed interpretation of them is still unclear. For instance, the parable of the mustard seed (Mk. 4:30–32) is a wonderful encouragement: from the tiniest beginnings, insignificant in the world's estimation, God's kingdom grows to mighty proportions. But what exactly does this encouraging message mean? Is Jesus predicting that the church will grow and grow throughout history, until it becomes a mighty force for good in the world? Or is he saying that the church will always be weak and never reveal in this age the destiny awaiting it in the next? Should we apply this locally, and expect to see our own churches grow in this way; or should we always expect to experience weakness and insignificance, even alongside success and growth?

The answers to these questions are not provided by the parable. Part of having 'ears to hear' means (as we saw in chapter 2) that we have to provide our own meaning, interpreting the parables carefully in the light of our experience and our overall understanding of the Bible. It is just the same with Revelation and with 'apocalyptic' writing generally. It works at a very deep level in us, conjuring up images which evoke feelings and responses of adoration and praise – or of fear. We shall, of course, go on to ask questions of the 'What exactly . . .?' type, just as we did of the parable of the mustard seed. But we can be encouraged by that parable without receiving definite answers to any of our further questions. And so with Revelation: many puzzles may remain, but it is still a most inspiring book.

The word 'apocalyptic' means 'unveiling' or 'revealing'. Revelation is called the 'Apocalypse' in Greek. While Revelation is the most prominent piece of apocalyptic literature in the Bible, there are many other examples, both in the Old and the New Testament. In the Old, the book of Daniel stands out, but the apocalyptic style is found throughout the prophets (see *e.g.* Am. 8:9–12; Joel 3:12–16; Is. 34; Ezk. 1; 8 – 11; 40 – 48). The style developed greatly during the period between the Testaments, when fascinating works like the *Apocalypse of Enoch* and the *Sibylline Oracles* were written. These provide a most important background to the apocalyptic literature of the New Testament, even though they are not 'Scripture'. In fact, Jesus himself used an apocalyptic style; his famous teaching about the destruction of the temple and the end of the age is full of apocalyptic language (Mk. 13; Mt. 24; Lk. 21). And there are passages in Paul and Peter which also fall into this category (*e.g.* 1 Thes. 4:13–18; 2 Thes. 2:3–11; 2 Pet. 3:3–13).

These writings present us with special problems, and call on us to apply carefully right principles of interpretation. What are these? We shall tackle this question under the two headings of 'problems' and 'principles', and concentrate on Daniel and Revelation as we do so.

Problems

1. What on earth is going on?

The main problem we face in reading apocalpytic literature is unpacking the symbolism. Revelation is a colourful, noisy book, as a constant succession of bright images dances across the page. How should we deal with them? Let us take a particularly vivid (and difficult) example from chapter 9. As I read through Revelation that day at college, I remember being totally baffled by the description of the locust-like creatures which arise from the Abyss:

> The locusts looked like horses prepared for battle. On their heads they wore something like crowns of gold, and their faces resembled human faces. Their hair was like women's hair, and their teeth were like lions' teeth. They had breastplates like breastplates of iron, and the sound of their wings was like the thundering of many horses and chariots rushing into battle. They had tails and stings like scorpions,

and in their tails they had power to torment people for five months. They had as king over them the angel of the Abyss, whose name in Hebrew is Abaddon, and in Greek, Apollyon.

(Rev. 9:7–11)

What on earth is going on? The point is, of course, that nothing is going on *on earth*. John has been taken behind the scenes and is watching 'the seven angels who stand *before God*' (8:2) as they blow their trumpets. What he sees affects the earth and has tremendous relevance for those who live on it; but he is actually watching 'heavenly' events in the sense that the veil has been lifted and he is able to see the heavenly reality behind earthly events.

This is why his language is so extraordinary. In order to convey these unearthly realities, he piles up images and symbols from many different sources. In fact, John uses a new kind of Greek in Revelation; scholars have been puzzled by it, not recognizing it as a dialect known from any other source. It breaks all the standard rules of Greek grammar with great enthusiasm, although it has an inner consistency and logic of its own. The best explanation is that John knew he could not use language in any ordinary way to convey what he had seen. So he created a new style, which matches the creative use of symbolism throughout the book.

We shall try to apply the approach we worked out in connection with the imagery from Joel 2:31 (above, pp. 105–106). We need to take four distinct steps in interpretation. (1) Look at the overall context; (2) think about the background to the symbolism, especially within the Bible; (3) look at the way John develops the picture, using the traditions on which he builds; and (4) consider what the symbols actually mean, using our own spiritual 'ears' to listen with spiritual insight.

Step 1: look at the overall context. The locusts appear when the fifth angel blows his trumpet (9:1) and they form part of a series of judgments on humankind. In 8:13, the last three 'trumpet-blasts' are distinguished from the first four and announced as 'worse'. And whereas blasts one to four are all pictures of physical disaster on the earth, five and six are clearly demonic, involving the release of powers of evil. These locusts are like scorpions, able to inflict a pain so intense that those affected 'will long to die, but death will elude them' (9:6). But they are able to attack only those who have not been 'sealed' by God. We learned earlier that God has put his seal of ownership on his elect people, so that they are protected from judgments like those that follow the trumpet-blasts (Rev. 7:2–3).

Step 2: think about the background to the symbolism. The images of the swarm of locusts and of the scorpion sting are vivid and very real for all middle-eastern people. Some of John's readers might also have experienced the dreadful sight of a Roman army going into battle. They would certainly have no difficulty in imagining both the sight and the sound of a charging army.

But beyond these cultural images there are images drawn from biblical history. The series of plagues heralded by the trumpet-blasts reminds us very much of the plagues in Egypt, which included a plague of locusts (Ex. 10:1–20). As with Pharaoh, the purpose of these judgments is to create repentance (Rev. 9:20) – which they fail to do. The picture also draws heavily upon Joel, who ministered in the aftermath of a disaster caused by a swarm of locusts. He, too, compares the locusts with the horses of an invading army, describes them as roaring like chariots being driven into battle (Joel 2:4–5), announces their appearance with a trumpet-blast (2:1), and says that they have teeth like lions (1:6). He interprets the locusts as God's judgment and as his appeal for repentance (2:12–17). And the mention of 'the sound of their wings' (Rev. 9:9) reminds us of Ezekiel's vision of the heavenly throne borne along by four extraordinary 'living creatures', who also had human faces (Ezk. 1:10). He writes of them, 'I heard the sound of their wings, like the roar of rushing waters, like the voice of the Almighty, like the tumult of an army' (Ezk. 1:24).

John has not just reproduced the way these images were used earlier. He draws upon these Old Testament passages as he produces something new. So now we need to ask how he is using these images here. How does he go beyond these background elements? To answer this, we need to take the third step.

Step 3: look at the way the picture is built up. We notice that the picture is full of contrasts. On the one hand, these locusts look like horses (as in Joel) but they have human faces (9:7). They combine beauty and horror: women's hair and lions' teeth. They are demonic, but they wear 'something like' golden crowns, which we last saw on the heads of the elders around the throne in heaven (4:4). They make a noise similar to that made by the heavenly creatures around the throne, but they are from the Abyss, the abode of the powers of evil. John is careful to emphasize that they are not actually wearing golden crowns, but 'something like crowns of gold'. In other words, he presents these demons as counterfeits. From one angle, they look all right, even attractive. They come in human guise and seem to be glorified spiritually (golden crowns). But actually they are from hell, with power to torture all who are not protected by God's seal. Now we need to take a final step.

Step 4: consider what the symbols actually mean. Interpreters have a tendency to rush to this point without taking the necessary prior steps. Elsewhere in Revelation this can be a fatal mistake, especially when John's symbols are unpacked as references to definite historical people or events. Such interpretations may sometimes be correct, but jumping to an identification is not a way of short-circuiting this patient exploration of his symbolism.

The Jehovah's Witnesses make this mistake right here in Revelation 9. They interpret the trumpet-blasts as referring to the proclamations issued by the annual conventions of Witnesses held in the USA from 1922 to 1928 – one blast per year, calling down God's judgment on an apostate church and world. Consistently, they then compare themselves to the swarms of locusts sent upon the earth. Quite apart from the fact that this makes the meaning of the passage inaccessible to everyone who lived before the 1920s, such an identification ignores John's subtle use of symbols. What is more, the Witnesses hardly do themselves credit by comparing their proclamations (and themselves) to a demonic attack which disguises itself as angelic!

The interpretation of the symbols needs to grow out of the symbols themselves. Here opinions are bound to differ and John probably did not have one particular thing in mind. Such symbolism does not really *prescribe* interpretation; it *allows* it. Maybe we should say that John is thinking of everything which seems to offer life, but which turns to torture. We could find an example in drug-taking – so attractive to start with, but leading to addiction and degradation. Sexual freedom seemed to offer so much in the 1970s and 1980s, but now for many the torture begins as they discover they are HIV positive. The scorpion has stung. Others seek freedom by joining a sect or cult, only to find themselves trapped and longing for freedom again. Such deceptions, John tells us, are not just silly mistakes, but result from a demonic assault on the world.

But the angel was given the trumpet to blow by God (8:2). The demons came from the Abyss, but the Abyss was opened with a key supplied from heaven (9:1). Like the plagues in Exodus, these judgments appeal for repentance and so are part of God's Plan of salvation. They are not hopeless. The torture is only 'for five months' (8:10).

Carefully applied, these four principles will enable us to come to terms with apocalyptic symbolism wherever we meet it. We may only rarely feel that we have fully unpacked its meaning, but then that is exactly how we should feel. Just as so many of Jesus' parables aim to create an impressionistic likeness ('The kingdom of heaven is like a merchant . . .' Mt. 13:45, *etc.*), so does apocalyptic symbolism. What we should try to do is to sense rightly the likeness that Jesus, or the apocalyptic writer, sees.

2. Does the Bible predict the future?

For some interpreters the value of biblical apocalyptic literature lies chiefly in its power of prediction. It is well known, for instance, how some have found the European Union predicted in Revelation 13. And in some circles there is still eager expectation of an invasion of Israel from the north, as predicted in Ezekiel 38 – 39, and of the battle of Armageddon (Rev. 16:16). Similarly, Jehovah's Witnesses base their whole picture of the last things on Daniel, which they feel is being fulfilled in detail today.

The approach to apocalyptic symbolism which we worked out above will guide us through this question. There are three vital principles to observe.

First, *assume that the details are symbolic*. We should assume that the 'concrete' details of these visions are intended symbolically unless there are clear indications to the contrary. 'Armageddon' is a good example of this. John's readers would not recognize the name, for there is no such place on the map. It means (in Hebrew) 'mountain of Megiddo'. There certainly was a place called Megiddo, in the north of Israel, not far from Mount Carmel. But there was no mountain there! Zechariah, in fact, refers to 'the *plain* of Megiddo' (Zc. 12:11). So we are being prompted to reflect on the meaning of the name, rather than to interpret it as a physical location. What should we think?

- Megiddo is the place where the kings of the Canaanites assembled against Israel, only to be defeated by Deborah and Barak on a day when 'from the heavens the stars fought' (Jdg. 5:19–20). The 'stars' here picture heavenly forces that stepped in on the side of God's people.
- Mountains are often associated with God's judgment in the Old Testament. (See, for example, Ps. 144:5; Is. 13:4; 18:3, 6; 34:3; Ezk. 38:21; 39:4.)

The name 'Mount of Megiddo' therefore neatly expresses

symbolically the idea of God stepping in to exercise judgment on the pagan nations of the earth.

Secondly, *accept the visionary's interpretation*. Sometimes, the context can prompt us to interpret visions literally. This applies, I believe, to Daniel's visions of the future. He is supplied with the key to the interpretation of his own visions. In Daniel 7:17–18 he is told that the four great beasts he just seen 'are four kingdoms that will rise from the earth'. This looks back to the interpretation of Nebuchadnezzar's dream in Daniel 2, where a succession of four great empires was pictured, starting with Babylon, over which Nebuchadnezzar ruled (2:37–43). The fourth empire was to be overthrown and replaced by a kingdom set up by God himself (2:44).

As the book progresses, the identity of these later empires becomes clear. Belshazzar the Babylonian is replaced by Darius of the Medo-Persian empire (5:30–31), and then we discover that it, in turn, is to be overthrown by the king of Greece (8:20–21). This is precisely what happened when Alexander the Great swept out of the west in 332 BC (8:5) and overthrew the Persian empire in the course of a nine-year campaign which left him master of a huge empire stretching right across to India. Daniel is then given visions which unfold the history of this Greek empire: how it fell apart when Alexander died (8:8, 22; 11:4), particularly into northern and southern divisions. Chapter 11 describes in detail the complicated relations between these divisions, which we can easily identify as the rival dynasties of the Ptolemies in Egypt (south) and the Seleucid kings who ruled most of what remained of Alexander's empire in the north and east.

In particular, Daniel looks ahead to one king of the northern (Seleucid) dynasty, who will set himself up against the Lord and will cause the daily sacrifices in the temple to cease for a period of '2,300 evenings and mornings' (8:9–14; compare 11:31). This happened under the dreadful king Antiochus IV Epiphanes (175–164 BC), who terminated the daily sacrifices in December 167 and erected an altar to the Greek god Zeus on the site of the altar in the temple. Three years later the sacrifices were restored, following a revolt against Antiochus. The whole story is told in the first book of Maccabees, chapters 1 – 4, in the Apocrypha. There, the altar to Zeus is called 'the abomination of desolation' (1 Macc. 1:54), picking up Daniel's prophecy in 8:13 and 11:31.

The fulfilment of all these prophecies is so exact and clear that it is quite inappropriate to make the kings of the north and the south anything other than what they are – the Greek kings of Seleucia and Egypt respectively. Our knowledge of history guides us and inclines us to a literal interpretation of Daniel's visions. But we certainly do not exhaust his significance by pointing out how exactly his prophecies were fulfilled. The purpose underlying them is to show how 'the Most High is sovereign over the kingdoms of men and gives them to anyone he wishes' (4:17, 32). Whatever the ups and downs of God's people, and however confused this world's politics may be, he is in charge and will establish his kingdom over all! This is a tremendously encouraging message which comes across the centuries and speaks with great relevance to us in a world where a nuclear strike could destroy us all.

Thirdly, *interpret with Jesus in mind*. Looking beyond the turmoil of human politics, Daniel points to a further kingdom, to be set up by God himself and possessed by his people. Before that, further horrors are yet to come: a fourth kingdom will overthrow the Greek empire; it will be a fearsome kingdom which will 'devour the whole earth, trampling it down and crushing it' (7:23; plainly the Roman empire is meant). But then this final empire is to be overthrown, as 'one like a son of man' is invested with 'authority, glory and sovereign power' by God (7:13–14).

As we investigate the meaning of this overthrow of the fourth kingdom, a further vital principle of interpretation appears. Just as we interpret the symbolism of Revelation by referring back to the Old Testament, so we may interpret Daniel by referring forward to the New Testament and thinking of the fulfilment in Christ.

This is especially helpful because Daniel poses a problem which he leaves unsolved. Having presented in chapter 7 the 'son of man' through whom God's people will be given a kingdom which overthrows the fourth 'beast' (7:26–27), he then introduces in chapter 9 'the Anointed One, the ruler' who is to come (9:25). But, instead of ruling, this person will be 'cut off', and 'the city and the sanctuary' will be destroyed by another ruler (9:26), who will 'put an end to sacrifice' and cause further 'abominations' (9:27). Is this 'Anointed One' meant to be the same as the 'son of man' in 7:13? Why then is he cut off? Is this termination of the sacrifices, and the accompanying abominations, the same as those associated with Antiochus Epiphanes? But Antiochus did not *destroy* Jerusalem and the temple; he merely defiled it.

These puzzles are resolved as we turn to the New Testament. Jesus identified himself as the Son of Man; it was his favourite self-description. He proclaimed the arrival of the kingdom of God in and through himself (Mk. 1:15). As the Son of Man, he exercised kingdom authority (Mk. 2:10). But he also predicted his own death as the Son of Man (Mk. 9:31; 10:33, 45); and he foresaw a coming 'abomination of desolation' associated with the future destruction of Jerusalem and the temple (Mk. 13:1–2, 14). His prediction was horribly fulfilled just forty or so years after he spoke, first as Jewish Zealots desecrated the temple, and then as the Romans captured the city and destroyed it.

Daniel simply sets the 'son of man' who receives the kingdom, and the 'Anointed One' who is cut off, alongside each other without any attempt to resolve this strange contradiction. In Jesus, we see that it is not a contradiction at all, for he establishes the kingdom of God by going to the cross, to die for God's people there. No-one, reading Daniel 7, would have suspected that that was the route by which the son of man came to be presented to God and invested with kingship. But looking back from the vantage-point of the gospels, we can see how suitably they resolve the tension Daniel leaves unsolved. The Son of Man *is* the Anointed One.

There is still a puzzle, however. The power of the fourth beast was meant to be overthrown by the kingdom of God. But the Roman empire continued unconquered for centuries after Jesus. How can we understand this? Should we perhaps not try to pin Daniel down so precisely – or does this indicate that we have misunderstood him? Tackling this question brings us face to face with another problem of interpretation posed by apocalyptic literature.

3. The numbers game

Daniel and Revelation are full of numbers. Again, the vital principle is that the numbers are symbolic, even when they are also literal. There were literally seven churches which received Revelation (see Rev. 2 – 3), but 'seven' indicates completeness or wholeness, and it is clear that the seven actual churches in Asia Minor represent the whole church of Christ. The book of Revelation has a message for more than just the Christians at Ephesus, Smyrna, and the rest. The cycle of seven letters in Revelation 2 – 3 is the first of a series of 'sevens' – seals (chapters 6 – 8), trumpets (chapters 8 – 11), signs (chapters 12 – 14) and bowls (chapters 15 – 16).

'Twelve' is another significant number in Revelation. As the number of the tribes of Israel and of the apostles, it signifies the people of God. From this basic idea, multiples become possible. The 144,000 of Revelation 7:1–8 is a picture of the complete people of God, as elect and known by him, and 'sealed' to protect them from all harm upon earth (7:1–3; 9:4). John then sees the same people of God in heaven (7:9–17), this time 'a great multitude that no-one could count' (7:9). God knows the exact number of his people, even though it defies human computation (compare Lk. 12:4–7). So 144,000 represents an exact number, but is not the exact number itself.

The Jehovah's Witnesses have made a sad mistake in interpreting the 144,000 literally. They believe that God's people are divided into two groups, the 144,000 who reign with Christ in heaven, and the 'great multitude' who serve him in a paradise on earth. They maintain this literalism in spite of the fact that the Israelite tribes listed in 7:5–8 are clearly symbolic (as they are happy to agree). They also reverse the locations: in Revelation 7 the 144,000 are on earth and the 'great multitude' is in heaven.

Coming back to Daniel and the problem of the overthrow of the fourth empire, we find that we are again dealing with multiples of seven. Daniel remembers that Jeremiah had prophesied how long the exile in Babylon would last – seventy years (Dn. 9:2; Je. 29:10). When he himself had been in exile for some sixty-six years, Daniel felt prompted to confess the sins of God's people and to pray specifically for the end of the exile (Dn. 9:4–19). According to 2 Chronicles 36:22–23 and Ezra 1:1, his prayer was wonderfully answered, for in that very year Cyrus, the Persian emperor, issued a decree allowing the exiles to return. This was, in fact, less than seventy years after Jerusalem had been destroyed and the main bulk of the people carried into exile, which may explain why the author of 2 Chronicles gives the 'seventy' a symbolic interpretation as a 'sabbath' which the land enjoyed while the people were absent (2 Ch. 36:21).

Daniel, too, receives an assurance that such a decree will be issued (9:25). But this is not the main point of the reply that he receives. He is given a vision which looks far beyond a mere physical return from exile and takes seriously the real problem at the heart of his prayer – the sin of Israel. He is told that

> Seventy 'sevens' are decreed for your people and your holy city to finish transgression, to put an end to sin, to atone for wickedness, to bring in everlasting righteousness, to seal up vision and prophecy and to anoint the most holy.   *(Dn. 9:24)*

In other words, God has a far greater purpose than just an end to the exile. He has a plan for the whole future, which will come to fruition after 'seventy "sevens"' (or 'weeks'), when the problem of sin will finally have been dealt with. The verses

129

which follow (9:25–27) then contain the prophecy of the coming of the Anointed One. The point at which he is 'cut off' is placed at the end of the sixty-ninth 'seven'; in other words, nearly at the end, when God's whole Plan will be brought to completion (9:26). Throughout the final 'seven', Daniel is told, 'war will continue until the end'. But in the middle of this seventieth 'seven', the sacrifices will be terminated in Jerusalem (9:27).

Half a 'seven' is left over, but not forgotten. Right at the end of the book we discover that this was not accidental. Daniel asks when all his prophecies are going to be fulfilled, and receives the enigmatic reply:

> From the time that the daily sacrifice is abolished and the abomination that causes desolation is set up, there will be 1,290 days. Blessed is the one who waits for and reaches the end of the 1,335 days. *(Dn. 12:11–12)*

Because of the context here (looking back over all the prophecies of the book), it is best to take this as referring to the second abolition of the sacrifices, rather than to that under Antiochus IV Epiphanes. This is confirmed when we realize that 1,290 days is almost exactly three and a half years, equivalent to the missing half 'seven' from chapter 9. By changing the number to 1,335, Daniel manages cleverly to convey the idea of a period which is fixed in God's Plan, but which seems to run beyond its limit.

So the power of the fourth empire is to continue right up to the end, for a full 'seven' after the cutting off of the Anointed One, and for half a 'seven' after the destruction of the temple and the abolition of the sacrifices. Thinking carefully about Daniel in the light of the fulfilment that we actually find in the New Testament, we can see how perfectly it fits. From his perspective, we are living now in that last half 'seven', the period when 'Many will be purified, made spotless and refined, but the wicked will continue to be wicked' (12:10).

We can see, too, how it makes no sense to try to interpret

these numbers literally. Interpreting them in the light of Jesus, they simply do not fit if taken literally, quite apart from the fact that Jeremiah's 'seventy years' receive a symbolic interpretation within the Old Testament itself. They need to be treated as another particular element of apocalyptic symbolism.

Principles

Now we can look back over the ground we have covered, and summarize our approach to apocalyptic literature by listing four basic principles of interpretation.

1. Take the genre seriously

By 'genre', I mean the type of literature. We need to respect apocalyptic literature for what it is, and not require it to be something else. This has one very important consequence: we must interpret it in the light of its original historical setting and purpose, otherwise we shall end up simply imposing our own ideas upon it. John wrote Revelation not in order to predict the future, but to encourage Christians being persecuted for their faith, particularly in Asia Minor but also elsewhere. The encouragement consists of allowing them to see behind the scenes, to observe the powers that control the confusion of human history and, in particular, to realize who sits on the throne, sovereign over even the worst things that could happen to them. Because he was trying to communicate the incommunicable, John drew on the vast reservoir of rich biblical symblism into which we have dipped our toes in this chapter. We shall understand him only as we drink deep at the same reservoir, and then enter sympathetically into the situation of those to whom the revelation was originally sent.

2. Get help!

Yes, getting help is a fundamental principle of interpretation. We cannot interpret this literature on our own; in fact, having bright ideas about the interpretation of biblical apocalyptic has been the starting-point of several sects. We need to read it in fellowship with the wider church. There are many excellent books and commentaries which can open up to us the richness of the symbolism and which we need to use enthusiastically.

3. Interpret in the light of the rest of the Bible

This principle of interpreting a passage in the light of the whole Bible is one that we have already seen in practical operation. We have used the rest of the Bible to supply the key to the meaning of a passage, looking both back to the Old Testament and forward to the New. But this principle has a further dimension to it. It is possible to get apocalyptic literature out of proportion and to use it as the key to the rest of the Bible. Again, this is a sad error of the Jehovah's Witnesses. It must be the other way round! Our basic, theological understanding of God and the Plan must grow out of the easier parts of the Bible; then, secondarily, we may come to the apocalpytic parts to have our vision enlarged and hearts warmed.

4. Rejoice in the certain; be happy with the uncertain

I am not at all certain of the rightness of some of the interpretations I have presented in this chapter. At some points I am particularly conscious of using my 'ear', my sense of biblical truth, to guide me. At such points I must be unsure because I cannot trust my ear not to distort and misinterpret the sound. As I grow in Christian truth, maybe it will be possible to be more certain.

But, on the other hand, it would be wrong to give the impression that biblical apocalytic literature is terribly vague and unclear. In broad outlines, Daniel and Revelation are not hard to understand, as we approach them from the rest of the Bible, and they are very thrilling as well. They give us tremendous confidence in God's sovereign control of the earth and its history and destiny, however confused its events may seem. They assure us that he will establish his kingdom over all. And they impart a vision of God and of Christ, and of the great sweep of history, which stretches the mind and prompts adoration on earth to match that in heaven. And that is the most important thing of all!

'I wish I understood Paul!'

Grappling with the letters

'I wish I understood Paul!' I have often heard this exasperated cry. The letters of Paul are hard to grasp. I remember vividly the embarrassment I felt when an occasional church-goer once read a passage from Philippians during the service one Sunday. First, he got the reference muddled and read from Philemon instead. Secondly, he was reading from the King James version, and it became clear, as he stumbled along, that it was complete gibberish to him. It might as well have been in Chinese for all he understood of what he was reading!

I felt dreadful; not just because I was sympathizing with him as he struggled to make sense of King James English, and not just because I could see one reason why he was only an occasional church-goer! I felt awful mainly because Paul is *not* incomprehensible, and it seemed such a waste that this intelligent man should go away with the impression that being a Christian means pretending to understand antique gobbledegook. Yes, Paul is difficult in parts; but no more so than any other part of the Bible.

Somone else's correspondence

The vital thing is to realize what these letters are. They are ordinary, personal communications between Paul (or Peter, James or John) and some of the earliest groups of Christians. When we read them today, we are in fact reading someone else's correspondence. Suppose you stumble across some old letters in your grandmother's loft, perhaps while sorting out her things after her death. You realize that she wrote them to your grandfather before their marriage. Intrigued, you begin to read them. The language is not difficult, yet they are hard to understand. She talks about things familiar to them but not to you; she uses 'in' language and jokes, gives advice without referring to the problem (because there was no need to), and casually mentions other people's affairs and doings. In fact, her letters make you feel as though you are eavesdropping through a closed door on puzzling snatches of private conversation.

That is precisely what we are doing when we read the New Testament letters. Each was prompted by particular circumstances affecting the people addressed. Sometimes the letter makes these circumstances clear, but not always. The letters are 'events' in a much longer story, that of the relationship between the authors and their readers. In writing to the Corinthians, Paul does not pause to summarize the long and fascinating story of his relationship with them so far, yet everything he says to them arises out of that story. That story forms the 'context' of the letter.

The need for research

If you decided to investigate your grandmother's letters further, you would have to discover her 'story'. You would need to know where she lived, what she did, who her friends were, what her hobbies and activities were, and particularly how she met your grandfather, and the course of their romance. The more you discovered about all these things, the more her letters would make sense. And if you managed to turn up some of his letters to her, you would be able to understand her replies much better. It is just the same with the New Testament letters. The more we can discover about both the writer and the readers, the more the meaning of the letters will become plain. It is easy to jump to false conclusions when you know only part of the story.

When we discover this kind of background information, we are able to exclude false interpretations. Suppose your grandmother mentions a trip to Scarborough in one of her letters. Knowing that Scarborough was a popular holiday resort, you assume that she went there on holiday. But reading on through the correspondence, you gather that her grand-parents ran a business there. Your interpretation of the earlier reference is clarified: you still do not know why exactly she went, but you can be fairly sure that the primary purpose will have been to visit her grandparents, rather than just to have a holiday. Then, in another letter, she mentions that she was 'run off her feet' in Scarborough. You are probably right in thinking that she was not running a marathon around the town, but helping her grandparents in their shop. Each further reference helps to limit the possibilities of meaning in the other references.

It is the same with the New Testament letters. The more we can gather about the real-life situation of both the writer and the readers, the nearer the truth we shall get, as various possible interpretations are excluded by our growing understanding. Here are two examples.

1. A stay in Rome

For many years, it was assumed that Romans was not really a letter at all, but a statement of the gospel, written in abstract terms. In contrast to 1 Corinthians, which clearly sets out to tackle problems in the church at Corinth, Paul apparently does not refer directly to the Romans' needs until chapter 14. So people believed that Romans was Paul's summary of his gospel, perhaps written basically for his own sake, and then sent to Rome just to prepare the church for his visit to them (see Rom. 15:23–24, 28–29). Scholars of a previous generation liked to treat

Romans as a kind of theological handbook. One of the sixteenth-century Reformers called it 'a compendium of Christian doctrine' – an apt summary of the general attitude to it. One modern scholar has called the letter 'Paul's last will and testament.' Pointing out that Paul wrote it on the eve of his journey to Jerusalem, he suggests that Paul did not know whether he would survive the trip, and wanted therefore to put down a clear summary of his gospel as a kind of bequest to the church.

But there is now a widespread feeling among other scholars that this is not the whole story. Paul does not touch on some things which, if it was a summary of his teaching, we might have expected to be there. For instance, he does not mention the church at worship or, in particular, the Lord's Supper. Nor does he deal with the second coming of Christ. In addition, we cannot ignore 14:1 – 15:12, where he certainly tackles some particular problems among his readers. He refers to a dispute between 'the weak' and 'the strong', and it is hard to know who these groups might be, unless they are rival groups in the Roman church. Other parts of the letter, too, suggest 'real events' in the background. In 3:1–8 he quotes a string of accusations made against him by Jewish Christians, and these are clearly still in mind in 6:1. In fact, they seem to underlie his whole presentation of 'justification by faith' in chapters 3 – 6. In 13:1–7, a little section of instruction on the Christian attitude to the secular state and the paying of taxes suddenly appears, and we naturally wonder why he puts it in. And then there is the question: why did Paul send it to Rome, a church he had never visited? We might have expected him to make it a circular letter if it was a summary of his teaching.

Putting together all these thoughts and observations, with all that we know of Paul's and the Romans' situation from elsewhere, it looks as though Romans is addressed to real, practical problems in the church there. The relevance of what Paul is writing was clear to his readers, without it being spelled out. For instance, we know from the Roman historian Tacitus that there was a tax revolt in Rome, just prior to the date when it is most likely that Romans was written. The tax system in Rome was the same as in Palestine; that is, people like Zacchaeus (Lk. 19:1–10) bought the right to collect taxes and were then allowed to collect as much as they liked, beyond what the state actually expected to receive. The abuses had become so great that, in AD 57, there was a general uproar in Rome about it, which doubtless included calls to withhold payment. In this situation, Paul's teaching about the Christian responsibility to pay taxes and to submit to the 'powers that be' (Rom. 13:1–7) becomes highly relevant. We are able to exclude the view that this is just a piece of general advice which might not be applicable if the taxes are unjust.

In fact Paul's comments about 'the weak' and 'the strong' in chapters 14 – 15 help us to reconstruct the whole background to the letter, so that we can read between its lines. We gather that Jewish and Gentile Christians were finding it difficult to come to terms with their varying backgrounds, and were criticizing each other for observing or not observing the Old Testament festivals and food laws (14:1–12). An argument like this could not be settled easily, because it involved so much theology. The Jewish Christians could point to the Old Testament commands to support their viewpoint. The Gentile Christians, on the other hand, could point to the fact that they had not been required to start celebrating Jewish festivals when they became Christians, either by Paul or by the Holy Spirit. They may have gone on to argue that Israel and the law had lost their special place in God's Plan, because of the Jews' general rejection of Jesus. In response, some Jewish Christians may have developed a deep suspicion of Paul for (apparently) teaching his Gentile converts to reject the Old Testament law.

This argument would have raised all the thorny questions that Paul tackles in Romans 1 – 11:

- ▶ the continuing validity (or not) of the Old Testament law (especially chapters 3 – 4, 7);

- whether Israel is still the chosen people of God (especially chapters 9 – 11); and
- the basis on which Gentiles have been admitted to God's people; why don't they have to become Jews (especially chapters 2 – 3, 5, 10)?

So, in a sense, Romans is a book with the answers at the back. When we discover something about the church in Rome, we realize that the letter is not cool and abstract, divorced from the immediate concerns of its readers, but right up to the minute. Our first impressions were deceptive.

2. A spell in Ephesus

Ephesians provides us with another example of the way in which we can limit the range of possible interpretations as we become more aware of the situation behind the letter. Current research is broadening our understanding of the Bible all the time.

The Crossway Bible Guide on Ephesians makes use of some research recently undertaken by a young American scholar named Clinton Arnold, at Aberdeen University. His discoveries have been published in his book *Ephesians: Power and Magic* (Cambridge University Press, 1989). He noticed that Ephesians uses words like 'power', 'strength', 'might', 'authority' and 'dominion' far more than the other letters, and presents a uniquely 'cosmic' picture of Jesus and the church. So he looked into the background of the 'power' language in Ephesians, and discovered that these words were widely used in magical spells and incantations at this time, and that Ephesus, in fact, was a centre for occult practices and magic arts. Many such spells have been found in Egypt, where the dry sands have preserved the fragile papyrus on which they were written.

Furthermore, the worship of the goddess Artemis at her huge temple in Ephesus (one of the seven wonders of the world) had a strongly occult dimension to it. She was called (among other things) *kosmokrator*, 'world-ruler', which is the very word that

Paul uses in Ephesians 6:12 ('our struggle is ... against the powers of this dark world', literally 'the world-rulers of this darkness'). By 'naming the names' of deities and spirits like Artemis, practitioners of these occult arts tried to tap spiritual power and bend it to their own uses. There were certain special names they could use, actually known as the 'Ephesian letters'.

Many of the Ephesian Christians had been converted out of occultism. Luke tells us this in Acts 19:13–20, when he describes how 'a number who had practised sorcery brought their scrolls together and burned them publicly' (Acts 19:17–19). Even though many of them took this step of renunciation, the fear of the powers they once sought to harness must have remained, especially if they found that pagan enemies were casting spells against them. And some of the new believers may have been tempted to adopt a 'belt and braces' approach, continuing to wear charms and amulets and trying to combine their Christian faith with their old practices. Some may even have regarded 'Jesus' as a new and extra-powerful 'name' to add to their magic armoury. This is certainly what the Jewish exorcists described by Luke in Acts 19:13–16 were doing.

Against this background, Paul's language in Ephesians 1:19–21 takes on a new meaning. He prays that the Ephesians may know

> ... the immeasurable greatness of [God's] power in us who believe ... which he accomplished in Christ when he raised him from the dead and made him sit at his right hand in the heavenly places, far above all rule and authority and power and dominion, and above every name that is named, not only in this age but also in that which is to come ...
>
> *(Revised Standard Version)*

This must have been a powerful message for the Ephesians, and deeply relevant to their situation, confronted daily as they were with the evidence of occult powers around them. Jesus is not just one of the 'names' that can be 'named', but is supreme over every other authority or power. Paul goes on to tell them how, in Christ, the Ephesian believers have likewise been raised to that same position, delivered from their former obedience to 'the ruler of the kingdom of the air', and equipped now with God's whole armour for the battle against their spiritual enemy. He even compares the church to a temple: Artemis may be a wonder of the world, but she cannot hold a candle to the temple that is rising around Jesus Christ, the 'chief cornerstone'. God himself lives in this temple by his Spirit (Eph. 2:19–22).

We just hear one side of the conversation as we read the New Testament letters. Through their research, people like Clinton Arnold enable us to understand the whole exchange. We can now see clearly how relevant Ephesians is to Christians facing the powers of evil in their more tangible forms. But actually this can already be sensed by spiritually minded Christians – just as you might have suspected, before you came across confirmation of it, that it was likely that your grandmother went to help in the shop in Scarborough, rather than just holiday there.

And, of course, Ephesians has a wider message than just 'how to cope with the occult'. Even though it seems to have this particular practical focus, Paul bases his message on a panoramic presentation of God's purposes and Plan for the world, which can speak deeply to Christians who are not having to deal with the occult. Similarly, all the New Testament letters can speak to us, even though we are eavesdropping and may never be aware of all the factors which shaped the 'meaning' of these letters originally. We can gather enough from the Bible itself, and there are plenty of commentaries and other aids to help us deepen our knowledge.

Following up these thoughts, we can now focus on four principles which are vital in handling the New Testament letters today.

Handling the letters today

1. Read them as conversations

This first principle, of reading the letters as though they were conversations, applies what we have been thinking about so far. In some cases they really are conversations, in that they are written in direct response to letters or other communications from the recipients. 1 Corinthians is the clearest example of this. Paul has had a letter from them (1 Cor. 7:1), and he has also heard directly about them from visitors (1:11), and both sources of information prompt his reply. As he moves from subject to subject – 'Now about food sacrificed to idols . . . Now about spiritual gifts . . . Now about the collection . . .' (8:1; 12:1; 16:1) – it looks as though he is going through a list of questions they had asked in their letter. At the same time, however, he is clearly incorporating into his answers far more than they were expecting. He responds to what he has heard about them as well (see 11:18), and anticipates objections and comments from them as he writes, as if he were actually talking to them face to face (see 15:35). This probably explains why Paul employs a speaking style as he writes. He addresses them directly, uses lots of rhetorical questions, and even gets sarcastic (4:8). He writes as though he were actually present with them.

This unfortunately means that, occasionally, we simply do not know what he is talking about. In 1 Corinthians 15:29, for instance, he refers in passing to the strange practice of 'baptizing for the dead'. Presumably the Corinthians knew what he was referring to!

Similarly, what he writes in 1 Corinthians 7:36–38 about marriage is unclear, because we do not know exactly what the Corinthians had asked him. Paul could be referring to fathers who did not know whether they should give their daughters in marriage (NIV margin), or to engaged couples who were wondering whether to go through with their marriage (NIV text), or to married couples who were abstaining from sex for spiritual reasons and were wondering whether or not to continue in this way (New English Bible). Presumably, the Corinthians' letter (7:1) made clear what their particular problem was and they read his reply in the appropriate way. The ambiguity arises from our ignorance of the 'conversation'. This is no great problem, because it is likely that what Paul says would be applicable to all three possibilities, and the vital thing for us is the principle he is seeking to apply (which is that marriage is perfectly all right, but there are sometimes more important things for Christians to be doing than getting married).

Spotting the 'conversation' – that is, seeing how the writer is interacting with the situation of the readers – is a tremendous help in reading. 1 Peter sprang to life for me when I realized the kind of people Peter was writing to. He calls them 'strangers in the world, scattered throughout Pontus, Galatia, Cappadocia, Asia and Bithynia' (1:1). It becomes clear that the various scattered groups he addresses in this wide area were being persecuted or facing the real risk of it (see 1 Pet. 1:6–7; 2:12, 20–24; 4:12–19; 5:9–10). He repeats the idea of their being 'aliens and strangers in the world' (2:11), and those words have a clear political meaning. He is using 'aliens and strangers' as a metaphor; none of us is at home in this world, because we are really God's people (2:9), but many of Peter's readers were probably literal 'aliens and strangers'. They had no rights of residency, no vote and no right to own property or hold public office. Undoubtedly many of them were slaves, who added to all these debits the further one that they did not even own themselves.

In this situation of alienation, isolation, exploitation and persecution, Peter's words are fantastically encouraging. He points them to the sufferings of Christ who, like them, was rejected, but who through his suffering and death was victorious over the powers of evil (2:21–24; 3:17 – 4:1). He tells them that their suffering, too, is leading them towards a glorious heavenly inheritance already prepared for them (1:3–9; 5:10–11). And he assures them that, even though they have no home on this earth and are scattered and isolated, yet they are

... a chosen people, a royal priesthood, a holy nation, a people belonging to God, that you may declare the praises of him who called you out of darkness into his wonderful light. Once you were not a people, but now you are the people of God; once you had not received mercy, but now you have received mercy.   *(1 Pet. 2:9–10)*

Their spiritual situation is the exact opposite of their social position. This is thrilling, and gives 1 Peter a special relevance to Christians in similar situations today. It speaks, too, to all of us in so far as we suffer and feel ourselves to be the victims of forces beyond our control.

2. Clarify the problems tackled

It is important to read the text carefully so that we isolate the real problem being tackled. It is all too easy to read it quickly, gain a general impression of the subject under discussion, and then draw conclusions which do not actually tie up with what the writer really meant. Let us take another example from 1 Corinthians.

In 1 Corinthians 15:12 Paul refers to 'some of you' who 'say that there is no resurrection of the dead'. Then he goes on to insist that there *is* a resurrection, with Christ the first to be raised (15:13–20). At first sight it is difficult to see how anyone can be a member of the church, yet deny the resurrection. How is it possible to be a Christian and not believe in life after death?

Light is shed on this as we discover exactly what Paul has in mind. It turns out to be of great relevance to the public controversy which occasionally takes place today on the subject of the resurrection of Christ. Certain leading churchmen have caused suprise (and concern) by insisting that Jesus' resurrection was 'spiritual', not physical; they would not be upset if someone were able to unearth his grave and find a skeleton in it. They assure us that they are not denying the resurrection as such, but merely its mode, as traditionally understood. But in fact that is precisely the point at issue in 1 Corinthians 15.

In Paul's day there were very few people who denied all life after death. Most pagans believed in it (although, of course, ideas of what it was like varied considerably). So it is highly unlikely that some of the Corinthian Christians were denying it. If they were denying the resurrection of Jesus, Paul could not address them as members of the church at all, and would in any case have focused on this instead in 15:12. But we find that he is arguing from the resurrection of Jesus (which presumably these people accepted) to prove the resurrection 'of the dead' (which they denied). How could this be?

The answer comes when we discover something of the religious atmosphere which prevailed at the time. Many pagans then distinguished sharply between body (matter) and spirit, and it is clear that this distinction crept into the thinking of Christians too. Later, Christian groups calling themselves 'Gnostics' built whole systems upon this distinction because, when it is rigorously applied, it has a radical effect. The incarnation, for instance, becomes impossible: if bodies (matter) are evil or unclean, God would be defiled by taking on a human body. 'Gnosticism' did not appear until after the New Testament was completed. But some of the tendencies of thought which gave rise to it were already well established, for this distinction between matter and spirit went back to the early Greek philosphers, well before New Testament times.

Against this background, it becomes clear what these people were saying. They were not denying the resurrection as such, but merely the resurrection of the body. In fact, it looks as though they thought they had already risen from the dead and were enjoying the life of heaven. Paul refers to their view of themselves sarcastically in 4:8:

> Already you have all you want! Already you have become rich! You have become kings – and that without us!

Quite possibly they thought they spoke in the tongues of angels when the church met for worship (13:1). For some of them, this division between body and spirit may have meant that they felt it did not matter what Christians did with their bodies, because the body is of no spiritual account. Paul certainly saw the need to speak directly against sexual immorality on the grounds that

> . . . your bodies are members of Christ himself . . . Shall I then take the members of Christ and unite them with a prostitute? Never! *(1 Cor. 6:15)*

At any rate, it is clear that they were denying the resurrection of the body, on the grounds that the body does not matter and that Christians have already entered spiritual life in Christ. Paul takes this view to be a denial of the resurrection itself, because it must imply that Christ's resurrection also was merely spiritual. This, for Paul, meant no resurrection at all.

As a good Hebrew, steeped in Old Testament ways of thinking, he did not accept this distinction between body and spirit. We are whole beings, so that if there is to be resurrection it must touch the whole of us, body, mind and spirit. As the argument develops in 1 Corinthians 15, we realize that Paul is arguing for the resurrection of the *body*. When he quotes a possible objection to his argument in 15:25 ('But someone may ask, "How are the dead raised? With what kind of body will they come?"'), it is clear that he has met it before. It amounts to a scornful denial of the possibility of physical resurrection: 'How can the dead be resuscitated from their tombs? Will decomposed corpses be reassembled? Or will whatever remains come back to life? How ridiculous!' Paul roundly insists that he is thinking not of the resuscitation of corpses but of the resurrection of the whole person to a wholly new life, in which we shall receive 'spiritual bodies' in the likeness of the Lord Jesus (15:42–49). Just as a seed disappears in the ground and gives birth to something completely different from itself, yet continuous with it, so our bodies will die and disappear, only to become the seed for something ten times more glorious in God's hands.

So it turns out that Paul is opposing something very similar to the 'spiritual, not physical' understanding of the resurrection defended by these leading churchmen recently. In fairness to them, we must grant that their position is not exactly what Paul rejects so vigorously. But it is sufficiently close for us to be fairly sure of what he would say to them today.

Such direct application and relevance can grow only out of a patient study of the precise problems which were tackled in the New Testament letters.

3. Discover who the opponents are

Linked with this is the discovery of exactly who was opposing the letter-writers. This is particularly relevant to the letters of the New Testament, because here opponents are often confronted head on. 1 John gives us an interesting example. John warns his readers aginst 'the antichrist', who is 'the man who denies that Jesus is the Christ' (Jn. 2:22). This antichrist has caused a division in the church (2:18–19) and we may presume that an argument about Jesus lay at the heart of this. Again, we need to be as clear as possible about the two sides of the argument. John spells them out:

> Every spirit that acknowledges that Jesus Christ has come in the flesh is from God, but every spirit that does not acknowledge Jesus is not from God. This is the spirit of the antichrist . . .   *(1 Jn. 4:2–3)*

Many scholars think that John is referring to the view of a teacher named Cerinthus, who lived towards the end of the first century. Even if he is not personally in mind, his views fit the situation so well that it is hard not to take him as representing what John opposes. Cerinthus believed that 'Jesus' and 'the Christ' were separate beings; that Jesus was merely a good and wise man, until 'the Christ' (a heavenly spirit) descended on him at his baptism; and that 'the Christ' empowered him all through his ministry, but departed from him again just before his death, so that 'Jesus' died alone. Behind this view lay the distinction between spirit and matter we were just considering; for a heavenly spirit could not suffer and die, nor could it actually *become* flesh (see Jn. 1:14).

It would be possible to translate 1 John 4:2, 'Every spirit that acknowledges that Jesus is the Christ, come in the flesh, is from God' – that is, true spiritual teaching treats 'Jesus' and 'the Christ' as identical, and does not distance 'the Christ' from 'the flesh'. Similarly, 'the man who denies that Jesus is the Christ' (2:22) is not a Jew, denying that Jesus is the Messiah, but someone like Cerinthus, denying that Jesus and the Christ are the same person. John will have nothing of this! He insists that 'Jesus Christ' is one person, who has 'come in the flesh' and died upon the cross 'as an atoning sacrifice for our sins' (4:10).

We can see, then, how important it is to clarify the views opposed within the New Testament. There are many published resources to help open such things up. Why not set yourself a challenge? Read Philippians 3 and try to work out who are 'those dogs, those men who do evil' (3:2), whom Paul warns against. You can pick up clues throughout the chapter. The Crossway Bible Guide on Philippians by Ian Coffey will help, and so will any of the commentaries or Bible dictionaries we recommend at the start of the Bible Guides.

4. Read the letters as wholes

We tend to chop up the letters, like the gospels, and read them in little portions. We saw that the whole point of gospels is that they replace the previous jumble of unconnected stories and sayings circulating among the churches, with connected, orderly accounts in which each individual story or saying is given a proper home. Each gospel therefore needs to be read as a whole. The letters were not compiled in the same way, but the same point applies to them, because each letter usually has one overarching theme or purpose which holds it all together and gives each part its meaning. But it is very easy to lose sight of the wood for the trees by getting bogged down in individual verses or sections.

'Bogged down' is a good way to describe what often happens. We run into something that puzzles us, so we sit there, determined not to move on until we have slain the beast that blocks our path. But this is a mistake. It is much better to keep moving and to read the letters in large chunks, getting a sense of their overall sweep and a feel of their tone. After all, this is how they were written and how they were intended to be read.

It is clear that Paul usually wrote quickly, probably by dictation (see Rom. 16:22), and this helps to explain the 'spoken' style he uses. Composing in this way, he was driven along by the pressure of the message he wanted to get across, and each part of his letter followed on as he sought to achieve his overall aim. Sometimes the result looks rather jumbled, but, as soon as we begin to catch sight of the thought that gripped and compelled him, this impression will begin to disappear. The vital question to ask is: *why?* For instance, why does this passage follow that? Why does he introduce this thought first? Why does he put in what looks like a digression, before continuing his argument? Why does he choose this key word which keeps reappearing? As we wrestle with questions like these we shall gradually develop a sense of the whole, built up of all its parts.

I can just imagine the fuss that would have been caused if Tychicus, who brought a letter from Paul to the Colossian Christians, had insisted on treating it in the way we often treat the letters today. In the Church of England (my own church), a passage from one of the New Testament letters is read at every communion service, usually just ten to fifteen verses long. Imagine Tychicus arriving at Colosse, bearing a letter from Paul which he has carried all the way from Rome (Col. 4:7–8). The church assembles. Tychichus stands up and begins to read, 'Paul, an apostle of Christ Jesus by the will of God . . .' – only to snap the scroll shut in the middle of chapter 1 with 'This is the word of the Lord. Thanks be to God.' He would have had the whole church about his ears! It is a crazy picture; just as crazy, in fact, as our habit of doing precisely the same thing with these letters today.

Of course, the pressure of life dictates that, in daily Bible-reading, we usually have to tackle the letters in short sections. There is so much meat in them, anyway, that we can feed upon them a verse at a time. But this is really not the way they were meant to be read. As a change, why not set aside a little more time and read one of the letters right through once every day for a week or more? Doing this in different translations will give interesting comparisons, while doing it with the same translation will enable you to begin to soak it up, so that the words begin to take on a special flavour. Imagine yourself sitting with the first recipients, eagerly gathered to listen to the latest missive from the great apostle.

Reading the letters of the New Testament is a job for life. Because they are so closely related to real life, and to the practical job of being Christians in this world, our understanding of them will grow as we ourselves grow in the Christian life. So we need to keep digging away at them and expect that we shall never exhaust ways of applying them in a whole lifetime of reading. Again and again our own experience, especially our experiences of suffering, will open up new insights into the meaning of these lovely letters. We are launched on the same enterprise as their first readers: an adventure in the footsteps of Jesus. God's word to them will become God's word to us nineteen centuries later, even though the world is so outwardly different. The first recipients are our brothers and sisters in the Lord. As we stand alongside them in fellowship, learning what it meant for them to be the first witnesses to Christ, we shall find our experience chiming with theirs, and we shall learn alongside them too.

Praying the prayers of the Bible

Using the psalms today

We have probably all got 'favourite' psalms; ones which have spoken to us with special force at times of need, or on which we depend to help us praise God when we are feeling down. The psalms always seem to get to the heart of the matter. In some churches they have a special place in public worship. In the Church of England, for instance, a psalm is prescribed for every service, almost as though it gives an essential spiritual 'fix'.

But their use in worship is declining. We tend to go first to choruses and other hymns instead. Many of these are excellent, and are often based on psalms or other passages of the Bible. But sometimes the link is rather tenuous and, in many cases, they do not compete with the richness and beauty of the psalms themselves.

Should we use the biblical psalms in public worship? There are two good reasons for doing so. First, what we sing gradually shapes the way we think and feel about God. We get used to praising him with certain words and through certain forms, and these work away within us at a very profound level, moulding our 'image' and knowledge of him. So it is vital that we should be feeding on a wholesome diet as we worship. The psalms give us an enormously wide-ranging view of God; for instance, they sing not just about his love and mercy, but also about his truth, anger, and justice. They display him as loving father, creator and redeemer, but also as awesome and holy judge. They also give us a much wider range of emotional responses, both to God and to what we see around us in the world, than we normally allow each other to express.

Secondly, the psalms are the hymns, choruses and praise songs that were sung in the temple at Jerusalem. Our 'book' of Psalms is a collection of them, made over a long period. The earliest ones date from the period of the first temple, built by Solomon, so when we read or sing them we are transported back into the earliest worship of Israel. We catch the moods and sense views of God which were held by people who had recently settled into the land God had promised them, with Jerusalem as their centre.

Some might feel that the worship associated with such a place is too remote for us to bother with; and in any case it is pre-Christian. Shouldn't we sing Christian hymns, rather than Jewish ones? The answer to this depends on whether or not we believe that God was truly present in the temple. If he was not, then of course the religion of the temple has no claim on us. But the New Testament clearly teaches that the saints of the Old Testament knew God: they knew him because of Christ, being forgiven and justified because of the retrospective effect of his sacrifice. We are therefore one with them in worshipping the God whom they knew as Yahweh, Lord God of hosts, and whom we now know as the God and Father of our Lord Jesus Christ. Using the psalms expresses our membership of God's one, age-long people.

We do not need to dig very far into the psalms before discovering that they were written by people who really did know God. In fact, they knew him more intimately and clearly than I ever expect to, this side of glory. It is true that they lived in ignorance of the full extent of God's love for us in Christ, but they enjoyed a closeness of fellowship with him in that temple which we may covet deeply. Sometimes we meet something which looks like boastfulness in the psalms, but I believe it is not. For instance:

> Vindicate me, O LORD,
> for I have led a blameless life:
> I have trusted in the LORD
> without wavering.
> Test me, O LORD, and try me,
> examine my heart and my mind;
> for your love is ever before me,
> and I walk continually in your truth.
>
> *(Ps. 26:1–3)*

I freely confess that I cannot pray such a prayer! But this is simply to admit that I am a spiritual pigmy, compared to this psalmist. He knew that he enjoyed unclouded fellowship with God.

A psalm for all seasons

As with every part of the Bible, we need to use the psalms aware of their original setting and purpose. Here are some of the basic points to bear in mind.

Some psalms were clearly designed for *special occasions*, particularly occasions involving the king: a coronation, Psalm 2; a royal wedding, Psalm 45; a special procession into the temple, Psalm 24; when going into battle, Psalm 20; when defeated in battle, Psalm 44. Some seem to be devoted to themes suitable for several occasions, like Psalm 65, which could be sung either at harvest or when the seed was sown, or when the 'firstfruits' were presented (see Dt. 26).

Many of them are ascribed to *King David* in brief captions (seventy-three in all). Fourteen of these are headed by historical notes indicating when David composed them (Pss. 3, 7, 18, 30, 34, 51, 52, 54, 56, 57, 59, 60, 63, 142). The tradition that David was a singer is deeply rooted in the Old Testament (see 1 Sa.

16:23; 18:10; 2 Sa. 22; 23:1), and there is no substantial reason to question these ancient ascriptions. Some of the psalms clearly started life as personal prayers by David and then found their way into public use.

Others are ascribed to various *temple singers*, particularly Asaph and a group called 'the sons of Korah'. We can imagine that the collection was supplemented as time went by, in response to particular needs and occasions. Unfortunately, we do not know how the psalms were sung or how they fitted into temple worship.

Some were written with *visitors and pilgrims* in mind. Psalms 120 – 134 are all called 'A song of ascents', and appear to have been written for the use of pilgrims on their way to Jerusalem. We may imagine them being sung on the journey. Psalm 84 is another beautiful pilgrim psalm.

It seems likely that the psalms formed a *spiritual resource for worshippers*. People would travel to the temple for festivals or for personal and family reasons at times of crisis in their lives, either joyful or sorrowful. For instance, there would be a constant stream of people bringing the redemption offering for their firstborn children (see Ex. 13:12–13; 22:29; Nu. 18:15–17), and of women coming for purification after childbirth (see Lv. 12:6–8; Lk. 2:22–24). Doubtless these would be happy family visits. Others would be in Jerusalem to appeal for judgment to the king in some dispute, and would visit the temple to pray about their situation. Still others would be there to repent of some specific sin and to offer sacrifice to the Lord. Others again would be there for teaching, because the temple, with its staff of priests and Levites, was a centre of learning in the law. And then there would be the residents of Jerusalem and others just passing through, devout people like Anna and Simeon (Lk. 2:25–38) who would be there because they loved the place and the Lord and came with a hundred and one different needs, joys and longings.

The psalms fit this crowd. It is interesting that, when they give thanks or lament about something, the psalms are never specific so that we never know precisely what the cause of joy or sorrow is. This is true even for the personal psalms of David that are related to specific historical situations in the captions. It looks as though they were preserved precisely because, being general, anyone could use them and relate them to their own situation. We can imagine people choosing from the repertoire psalms that fitted their own needs, either to pray privately or to give to the temple singers to perform while they joined in.

If this picture is right, then the psalms were used in their original setting much as we use them today. When we read our own troubles or joys into them, we are using them just as they were intended.

Classifying the species

Dr John Goldingay helpfully summarizes the seven things which the psalms say to God:

- Please!
- Help!
- Sorry . . .
- Thank you!
- That's great!
- You're great!
- I love you.

These different kinds of address are spread across five main types of psalm: they can be classified as laments, thanksgivings, testimonies, expressions of trust, and teaching psalms. The psalmist encouraged worshippers to be absolutely honest with God and to express to him exactly what was in their hearts, whether joy or grief, complaint or trust. Sometimes, these different styles of address are mixed within the same psalm. For instance, it is challenging to see how prayer for deliverance often turns into praise for deliverance as a psalm progresses (see the change at, for example, Pss. 22:23; 31:21; 54:7; 69:30).

Some have thought that these might be two-part psalms, with the second part kept for a return visit to the temple to give thanks for answered prayer. But this seems unlikely, because there is a strong emphasis in the psalms on joy in adversity. This arises from the knowledge that God's 'steadfast love' for his people is constant and unshakeable. So even when we are in desperate situations, the psalms encourage us to thank God for the coming deliverance, because it is so sure.

Let us look at these five different types of psalm.

1. Passing through the valley of weeping (Ps. 84:6)

There are some heart-rending *laments* among the psalms, some of them without any hint of light at the end of the tunnel. Psalm 88, for instance, seems to have been written by someone suffering from clinical depression. Some laments accuse God of having broken his promises (see Ps. 44, especially verses 23–26). Psalm 89 is a disguised lament of this sort; the real point of the psalm is neatly concealed until it bursts out in verse 38 with the cry that God has not kept his covenant.

This honesty is very compelling. It sits alongside a deep commitment to the Lord as the God of the psalmist. The questioning never moves over into cursing. Psalm 74, for instance, begins, 'Why have you rejected us for ever, O God?' But in verse 12 we discover why the writer can speak to God likes this: 'You, O God, are my king from of old.' He has not abandoned his commitment to the Lord. In fact, he is so secure in his relationship with him that it is natural for him to pour out his questions and challenges to God, as well as his praises.

We meet a special kind of lament in Psalm 51, David's prayer of confession after his sin with Bathsheba. It is tremendously moving, opening the door on to true confession in such a profound way.

2. 'Praise the LORD, O my soul'

Psalms 103 and 104 both begin and end with this great shout of praise. Laments are balanced by *thanksgiving*. Many of the

psalms are devoted simply to giving thanks and to praising the
Lord for what he has done, either just for the psalmist, or for
Israel as a whole. Psalms 103 to 118 are all devoted to this
theme. Psalm 136 is a *responsive* thanksgiving, with a little
refrain which (presumably) everyone sang ('His love endures
for ever'), while the cantor or singers sang the first line of each
verse.

3. 'These things I remember as I pour out my soul' (Ps. 42:4)

That responsive psalm also illustrates a further feature of many
psalms, both laments and thanksgivings. Many of them are
what today we would call *testimonies*. The writer recounts
something from his or her experience, as a vehicle for praise or
prayer. Looking back into the past is a vital aspect of the
'spirituality' of the psalms. This looking back can be either
personal or corporate: the psalmist may tell of something that
the Lord has done for him personally (*e.g.* Pss. 18, 32, 34, 73), or
he may look back over the history of Israel and retell the story of
her redemption (*e.g.* Pss. 78, 80, 105, 114).

The two can come together, as, for instance, in Psalm 77. This
is a testimony psalm, in which the psalmist tells us of his
present distress (verse 2). As an antidote, he remembers first his
own past with God (verses 3–9), and then 'your miracles of long
ago' in saving Israel (verses 10–20). Psalm 22 is similar: in his
distress, the psalmist remembers his own previous experiences
of God (verses 9–10) and the way God saved 'our fathers' in the
past (verses 3–5).

Part of what it means to be real before God is to bring our past
before him (whether good or bad), and to remember what he
has done for us, and how we have become what we are.

4. 'God is our refuge and strength' (Ps. 46:1)

There are powerful expressions of *trust* in the psalms,
underlying all the prayers for deliverance and help. 'O LORD,
come quickly to help me!' (Ps. 40:13) is not the desperate,

hopeless appeal that we are prone to pray. It arises out of a calm and clear confidence in God, based on two things: past experience ('I waited patiently for the LORD; he turned to me and heard my cry', Ps. 40:1) and present knowledge ('You are my help and my deliverer', Ps. 40:17). This kind of trust is woven into all the other kinds of address, and can be an inspiration and encouragement to us.

5. 'Blessed is the man who . . .' (Ps. 1:1)

Some psalms are not so strongly directed towards personal experience; rather, they set out to *teach*. Of course all the psalms have a great deal to teach us; but some of them are specifically teaching psalms, in that they present things in more objective or abstract terms. Psalm 1 is a good example, contrasting the 'way' of the righteous with the 'way' of the wicked and pronouncing the 'blessedness' of the person who delights 'in the law of the LORD'. Other examples are Psalms 15; 19; 34:11–22; 37; 49; and the massive 119. Sometimes these are called 'wisdom' psalms, because they have quite a lot in common with the style of the book of Proverbs. But this style of writing is generally mixed in with the other styles; see Psalm 41, for instance, which begins as a teaching psalm but moves over into lament and trust. Psalm 119 is a teaching psalm, but it is written in testimony form and thus has a deeply personal feel to it.

Using the psalms today

Here are four basic principles we need to note when using the psalms for ourselves today.

1. On your own and with others

What is the best way to use the psalms: with others in church or individually in private prayer? The answer is, clearly, both. They were designed with both settings in mind, as personal prayers but for public use; for individual pilgrims to use with others in the temple. This balance between the individual and the corporate reflected the nature of Israel's salvation. God chose Israel, as a nation, to belong to him; but each individual Israelite had a responsibility to walk with the Lord in trust and obedience, come what may.

The same applies to us. Because we are children of God individually, we are members of the body of Christ, so our worship should also have these two dimensions to it. Our individual testimony and experience cannot be separated from that of God's people as a whole. As Paul puts it, 'If one part [of Christ's body] suffers, every part suffers with it; if one part is honoured, every part rejoices with it' (1 Cor. 12:26). We are not a vague collection of isolated individuals, but a body. Using the same prayers both privately and in public can be a potent signal of our close fellowship with one another and our openness to each other's needs and situations.

2. Make them your own

There is something for everybody here. As we saw above, we are not misusing the psalms if we read our situations into them. They were designed for that! And the collection seems to have been formed precisely so that every situation and need would be covered. However we are feeling, and whatever needs we have, it is highly likely that there will be a psalm to express it for us – and at the same time to shape the way we feel.

In order to apply the psalms to ourselves, we need to 'translate' them into our own situation. We need to undertake two kinds of 'translation'. First, we need to relate them personally to the experiences of our lives which match those of the people for whom they were written. Our experiences may be very different in detail, but in essence they will be the same, because human nature does not change. So we can compile a checklist of psalms for use in particular situations: for instance:

- In the morning, facing the day: 5, 91, 95
- In the evening, before sleep: 3, 131
- When feeling emotionally 'raw': 38, 55, 61

- When gathering for worship: 84, 100, 134
- When ill: 6, 41
- In depression: 42 – 43, 88
- In grief: 22, 69
- In repentance: 32, 51
- Giving thanks for deliverance: 18, 34
- On a country walk: 104
- When needing some moral determination: 15, 120
- When facing a challenge: 20, 127
- When in need of guidance: 25, 121

The second kind of 'translation' arises from the fact that we live after the coming of Jesus, and therefore know so much more about God, his salvation, and what it means to belong to him. This affects our use of the psalms. For instance, when the psalmists wanted to praise God for saving them, they looked back to the exodus from Egypt (see 78, 105). But we look back to an even greater deliverance, from sin and death through the cross. Yet we worship the same God, who intended the exodus as a foretaste of what he was to do through Jesus (see Jn. 6 or Heb. 3 – 4). We can therefore 'translate' such psalms from their Old Testament setting and read them in the light of our 'New Testament' situation.

We can apply the same principle to the many psalms that talk about 'enemies'. For instance, take Psalm 25:19–20:

> See how my enemies have increased,
>   and how fiercely they hate me!
> Guard my life and rescue me . . .

We might be able to do the first kind of 'translation' and apply these words directly to ourselves, if we are in a conflict situation or facing persecution. But we can certainly do the second kind of 'translation' and apply it to the devil and his 'spiritual forces of evil', in the light of Ephesians 6:1–20. As Christians, we are all engaged in spiritual warfare, and we can apply the psalms to our spiritual battles. We know much more than the psalmists about the enemies that oppose God's people.

This second kind of 'translating' is also basic to the next point.

3. Read them in the light of the King

Using the psalms in the light of what God has done for us in Jesus has a special aspect to it, in that so many of the psalms are by King David or are about the king. We are given an important clue about how we should read these psalms today by the New Testament authors' use of some of them. They do not hesitate to apply them directly to Jesus, as if they were prophecies of him. For instance, Matthew not only records how Jesus gasped the first words of Psalm 22 from the cross (Mt. 27:46), but he also tells how the crucified Jesus was mocked, in terms which also point to Psalm 22 (compare Mt. 27: 39–43 with Ps. 22:6–8). John points out that Psalm 22:18 was 'fulfilled' when the soldiers cast lots for Jesus' clothing at the foot of the cross (Jn. 19:24).

Similarly, in his Pentecost sermon (Acts 2:24–32), Peter applied Psalm 16:8–11 to Jesus. Psalm 69 is often treated in the same way. There are no fewer than eighteen quotations of, or allusions to, Psalm 69 in the New Testament, all of them dependent on the belief that the psalm is about Jesus. The most important quotations are at John 2:17; 19:28–29 (Jesus' words, 'I thirst'), and Romans 11:9–10; 15:3.

The belief behind all these quotations is that Jesus is the King, the son of David. Because he occupies the office that David held, he shares David's experiences as king more than anyone else. We may rightly apply the Davidic psalm to ourselves, as the worshippers in the temple did. But there was an aspect to David's experience that was unique, simply because he was the elect king of Israel, set on his throne by God himself (see Ps. 2), and Jesus alone matches him in this respect.

Amazingly, the unique aspect of David's experience is not royal pomp, power or position, but suffering; something that at first sight we share, both with him and with Jesus. But the New

Testament authors saw something unique in the sufferings of the Davidic king as depicted in the psalms of lament and some of the other royal psalms. David foreshadowed the pain of the one who would suffer and die in our place.

So we may follow the lead of the New Testament and find Jesus wherever 'the king' appears in the psalms. We have to make necessary allowances for the fact that David was an imperfect king. For instance, verse 5 of Psalm 69 should not be applied to Jesus: 'You know my folly, O God; my guilt is not hidden from you.' David could pray this prayer, but Jesus is greater than David. Peter makes a similar point about his quotation of Psalm 16 in his Pentecost sermon, but puts it the other way round. He argues that, because the psalm could not apply to David, it must apply to Jesus (Acts 2:25–32).

Yet with the rest of Psalm 69 we can follow the example of the New Testament and see it as picturing Jesus' perfect suffering, his unfaltering love for God, his trust in him in the face of death and the wonderful deliverance which came to him in the resurrection (see verses 29–36). Because we want to 'follow the example of Christ' (1 Cor. 11:1), we shall pray that when he calls us to suffer, we may suffer with the same trust that Jesus showed, and so make the psalm our own.

4. Know how to handle the cursings

Most of us wish we could ignore the cursings in the psalms, and in practice we often do. We find it disturbing when they curse their enemies, and express joy at their defeat. For example:

> You made my enemies turn their backs in flight,
>   and I destroyed my foes.
> They cried for help, but there was no-one to save them –
>   to the LORD, but he did not answer.
> I beat them as fine as dust borne on the wind;
>   I poured them out like mud in the streets.

> *(Ps. 18:40–42)*

May the table set before them become a snare;
    may it become a retribution and a trap.
May their eyes be darkened so that they cannot see,
    and their backs be bent for ever.

(Ps. 69:22–23)

May his days be few . . .
May his children be fatherless . . .
May a creditor seize all he has . . .
May no-one extend kindness to him
    or take pity on his fatherless children . . .
May this be the Lord's payment to my accusers.

(Ps. 109:8–20)

O Daughter of Babylon, doomed to destruction,
    happy is he who repays you
    for what you have done to us –
he who seizes your infants
    and dashes them against the rocks.

(Ps. 137:8–9)

If only you would slay the wicked, O God! . . .
Do I not hate those who hate you, O Lord,
    and abhor those who rise up against you?
I have nothing but hatred for them . . .

(Ps. 139:19–22)

This does not make soothing reading. We have no cause to feel superior, though, because we can so easily think such thoughts ourselves. Even so, from the perspective of what *ought* to be, we have to say that curses like these fall far short of Jesus' command, 'Love your enemies and pray for those who persecute you' (Mt. 5:44). One of the most puzzling features of these cursings is that they sit side by side with the most inspiring expressions of love and trust. This is true of all the passages quoted above. How should we handle such cursings? Three points help us here.

First, *the 'cursings' reveal the seriousness of sin and the reality of judgment*. What is wrong about them, from the New Testament perspective, is that they do not distinguish between personal vengeance (and the desire for it) and divine judgment. The New Testament certainly does not give up the idea of divine judgment. On the contrary, we are told to expect 'the day of God's wrath, when his righteous judgment will be revealed' (Rom. 2:5). But at the same time we are told, 'Do not take revenge, my friends, but leave room for God's wrath, for it is written, "It is mine to avenge; I will repay," says the Lord' (Rom. 12:19). We can identify with the 'cursing prayers' of the psalms to the extent that they arise from a deep sense of the seriousness of sin and the need for divine judgment to establish right in the world. But we must not move from hating the sin to cursing the sinner. Jesus forbids it.

We get a hint of this in the last of the psalms quoted above. In the middle of a most moving statement of his love for God, the psalmist bursts out with this expression of hatred for those who hate the God he loves. We can understand this. And we can well believe that if he heard the God he loved telling him to love his enemies (as we have), then he would gladly obey.

Paul gives us a lead here, because he actually quotes the second passage above (Ps. 69:22–23) in Romans 11:9–10. He applies it to the unbelieving Jews by whom Jesus was crucified; he knows that judgment is inevitable for that act. But at the same time he expresses his deep grief over the Jews' unbelief and his intense longing that they should be saved, even to the extent of offering to stand under judgment in their place (Rom. 9:1–3; 10:1).

Secondly, *the 'cursings' arise from an 'exclusivism' which Jesus has ended*. Many of the psalms paint a thrilling picture of a world that has been saved and brought to recognize and worship the God of Israel (*e.g.* 47, 48, 66, 67, 82, 96 – 100, 108, 110). But often this is presented in terms of Israel's victory over the rest of the world. For instance:

> Clap your hands, all you nations;
>> shout to God with cries of joy.
> How awesome is the LORD Most High,
>> the great King over all the earth!
> He subdued nations under us,
>> peoples under our feet.
> He chose our inheritance for us,
>> the pride of Jacob, whom he loved.
>
> *(Ps. 47:1–4)*

The nations are seen as the natural enemies of Yahweh, the God of Israel (see also Ps. 2:1–3). Their defeat confirms that he has chosen Israel to be his 'inheritance', his special people. In Jesus this vision of a world brought to worship God has been fulfilled, but not by the defeat of the nations. It has come about by opening the doors to all comers, by faith. Jesus has died for his enemies (Rom. 5:10), so that

> If you belong to Christ, then you are Abraham's seed, and heirs according to the promise. *(Gal. 3:29)*

Far from being subdued by Israel, Gentiles are incorporated into Israel, spiritually. This is a great shift of emphasis; the enemies of God and his people are not *defeated*, but *won* by suffering love.

Thirdly, *our enemies are now spiritual, not physical.* We touched on this above when considering how to 'translate' the psalms into our situation. There is a place for cursing in the Christian life: we are to curse the devil and all his works, to renounce his influence over us, and to fight with the whole armour of God against all his devices (see 2 Cor. 10:3–4; Eph. 6:10–20; 1 Pet. 5:8–9). We are to 'beat' and subdue, not God's enemies, but our own bodies, which might stop us from winning the prize in the race (1 Cor. 9:24–27); see also Heb. 12:1–13; Rom. 8:12–14). So just as we 'translate' what the psalms say about the exodus from Egypt by applying it to the cross, so we do the same for the enemies who are renounced and cursed in the psalms. In fact, it was the exodus that separated Israel from the nations and created 'enemies', so these two features of the psalms go together in the long run.

We are doing for the psalms just what we decided was right for laws of the Old Testament: reading them through Jesus, in the light of their fulfilment in him. As we do this, our walk with him will be deeply enriched and we shall begin to grow into the same knowledge of God out of which the psalms were first written. Our understanding of them is 'fleshed out' (literally) by him.

The wisdom of the righteous

The writings of the 'wise men'

When did you last hear a sermon on a text from Proverbs, Ecclesiastes or the Song of Songs? As far as I can remember, I have never preached from any of these books, and only once or twice from Job, the fourth member of the group of books we look at in this chapter. So I have done nothing to reverse their neglect by Christians today. We tend to think of them as being on the fringes of the Bible, not central to its message. Some Christians have even been rather offended by them. The Song of Songs, for instance, is very sexy, and, at first sight, the two lovers don't seem to be married! And Ecclesiastes teaches that life is meaningless, which seems hard to reconcile with a Christian outlook on things. It is not suprising that they tend to be relegated to the sidelines. But together, these books form one of the Old Testament's three main streams of writing. In Jeremiah 18:18 we read:

> . . . the teaching of the law by the priest will not be lost, nor will counsel from the wise, nor the word from the prophets.

Here 'counsel from the wise' is set alongside the law and the prophets as a third form of teaching and revelation within Israel. The books of Proverbs, Ecclesiastes, the Song of Songs and Job form 'the counsel of the wise' within the Old Testament.

Such counsel was highly valued in Old Testament times, and we ought to question our neglect of this biblical tradition. As with all the types of writing in the Bible, we need to discover and apply the right techniques of interpretation. When we do so, we shall discover what a rich and life-enhancing message these wisdom books have for us as Christians.

'Wisdom' in Israel

We need to think about the background to these books in order to give ourselves a handle on them. 'Wise men' (and women) were held in great esteem. In 2 Samuel 14 we meet a wise woman from Tekoa who had a real influence on King David. He had other counsellors on his permanent staff (1 Ch. 27:32–33), and one of these was so highly regarded that it was said, 'The advice Ahithophel gave was like that of one who enquires of God' (2 Sa. 16:23).

The wisdom writings of the Old Testament look back chiefly to Solomon as their source and inspiration. We read of him:

God gave Solomon wisdom and very great insight, and a breadth of understanding as measureless as the sand on the seashore. Solomon's wisdom was greater than the wisdom of all the men of the East, and greater than all the wisdom of Egypt. He was wiser than any other man, including Ethan the Ezrahite – wiser than Heman, Calcol and Darda, the sons of Mahol. And his fame spread to all the surrounding nations. He spoke three thousand proverbs and his songs numbered a thousand and five. He described plant life, from the cedar of Lebanon to the hyssop that grows out of walls. He also taught about animals and birds, reptiles and fish. Men of all nations came to listen to Solomon's wisdom, sent by all the kings of the world, who had heard of his wisdom.

(1 Ki. 4:29–34)

This passage illustrates three important features of wisdom.

1. Solomon's special position

Ecclesiastes and the Song of Songs are both ascribed to Solomon, and so are large sections of Proverbs. There is no need to deny Solomon's authorship of these books, although they may have been edited a little by later wise men. 'Song of Songs' was the name given to the book in its Hebrew and Greek versions, though we sometimes refer to it as the 'Song of Solomon'. As Solomon wrote 1,005 songs, this one must have been regarded as the best of the lot!

Proverbs, although ascribed to Solomon as a whole, is actually a collection of sayings from different authors. The proverbs of Solomon begin at 10:1 (see the heading there). Proverbs 22:17 – 24:22 and 24:23–34 are two further collections of 'sayings of the wise'. There is a further section attributed to Solomon (25:1 – 29:27), then some 'sayings of Agur' (30:1–33) and some 'sayings of King Lemuel' (31:1–9).

2. The international nature of 'wisdom'

In 1 Kings 4 Solomon is compared to the internationally famous wise men of other nations, especially Egypt. There was a kind of international traffic in wisdom. The Queen of Sheba, for example, came to see Solomon because she had heard of his wisdom, and he 'answered all her questions; nothing was too hard for the king to explain to her' (1 Ki. 10:3). We discover more about this international traffic when we compare some of the wisdom writings of other nations with those of the Old Testament. There are many close parallels. For instance, many of 'the sayings of the wise' recorded in Proverbs 22:17 – 24:34 are also found in an Egyptian work called *The Teaching of Amenemope*, which was written around 1200 BC.

Since Israel regarded herself as being very different from the other nations because of God's special covenant with her, this sharing of wisdom is remarkable. How can we explain it? The answer is to do with the content of wisdom literature.

3. The special content of 'wisdom'

1 Kings 4:33 focuses on Solomon's understanding of the natural world, both plant and animal life. We see what is meant by this when we look at the wisdom books. It wasn't a 'scientific' interest in the sense that Solomon simply wanted to know how things worked. It was more than that. The wise man would see what happened, would explain it, and then reflect on what it tells us about the world. It was this last step which was the really vital one. Sometimes this could be something quite simple, like drawing a moral lesson:

> Go to the ant, you sluggard;
>   consider its ways and be wise!
> It has no commander,
>   no overseer or ruler,
> yet it stores its provisions in summer
>   and gathers its food at harvest.
>
> *(Pr. 6:6–8)*

Or an observation could be used as the basis for a comparison that would make people stop and think:

> Better to meet a bear robbed of her cubs
>   than a fool in his folly.
>
> *(Pr. 17:12)*

Or it might mean painting a panoramic view of the world around, and pointing out the wisdom and power of the Creator, alongside our helplessness to do anything about the evil and injustice that surround us. This is the great teaching of the magnificent closing chapters of Job (38 – 41), where we get just such a panorama.

This points us to the main thrust of these wisdom writings: they are to do with practical living and the pursuit of happiness, what life is all about at grass-roots level, and how to come to terms with the world and understand our existence on this earth. As Derek Kidner puts it in his Tyndale Commentary on Proverbs (IVP, 1964), these books move away from statements about God and his purposes (such as we find in the law and the prophets) to questions of many different types. There are 'What?' questions, such as:

- What are the dangers of immorality?
- What are the qualities of a good wife?
- What is the way to peace and happiness?
- What sort of person should a good king be?
- What are the essentials for human love at its best?

For answers to these questions we look especially to Proverbs and the Song of Solomon. Then there are deeper 'How?' and 'Why?' questions, such as:

- How can I come to terms with human suffering?
- Why do the righteous suffer, while the wicked prosper?
- How can I make the most of an existence I can't understand?
- Why am I on this earth at all?

These are the ones faced in Job and Eccelesiastes.

Israel could share a wisdom tradition with her neighbours because the questions they were asking were universal human questions, and wise men in every nation wrestled with them. As we shall see, neither Old Testament religion nor the fuller revelation of God in Christ provides final answers to all these questions. The world is still a very puzzling place. Why has God decided to make it the way he has? How do we reconcile the presence of evil in the world with the sovereign control of a good Creator? What are the biggest snares to avoid on this earth, and why are the most precious relationships often the ones that hurt us most? What is the best way to live in a complex and puzzling world? These questions 'bugged' people 3,000 years ago as much as they do us today. The wise men of many nations and religions got together to chew them over and, in just the same way, Christians today can find help from secular philosophers and psychologists in continuing to wrestle with them.

We might also find help from the adherents of other religions, as Israel's wise men did. They engaged in dialogue with the wise men of Egypt, without in any way compromising their faith in Yahweh, the God of Israel. We can do the same. What is needed is the recognition that, facing these deep questions, we are all in the same boat. The quest for answers continues.

The best way to set out some principles for unlocking wisdom literature today is to look through each of these four books in turn.

Proverbs: wisdom from the Lord

In the main section of the book (chapter 10 onwards), the proverbs come thick and fast without any apparent arrangement under different subjects. They are astute observations on human character and society: pithy, humorous, tragic or full of pathos. Some of them have become 'proverbs' in English:

> Pride goes before destruction,
>   a haughty spirit before a fall.
>
> *(16:18)*

> As a dog returns to its vomit,
>   so a fool repeats his folly.
>
> *(26:11)*

Some of them make us laugh because they hit the nail so neatly on the head when they observe some quirk of human behaviour:

> Like one who seizes a dog by the ears
>   is a passer-by who meddles in a quarrel not his own.
>
> *(26:17)*

> The sluggard says, 'There is a lion outside!'
>   or, 'I will be murdered in the streets!'
>
> *(22:13)*

If a man loudly blesses his neighbour early in the morning,
  it will be taken as a curse.

(27:14)

Others comment perceptively on the complexities of human character:

> Many a man claims to have unfailing love
>   but a faithful man who can find?
>
> *(20:6)*

> A heart at peace gives life to the body,
>   but envy rots the bones.
>
> *(14:30)*

> The purposes of a man's heart are deep waters,
>   but a man of understanding draws them out.
>
> *(20:5)*

And there is a deep awareness of the practical value of good qualities of character:

Better a patient man than a warrior,
  a man who controls his temper than one who takes a city.

(16:32)

Alongside these observations of character there is some pointed social comment:

> A poor man's field may produce abundant food,
>   but injustice sweeps it away.
>
> *(13:23)*

> Better to be lowly in spirit and among the oppressed
> than to share plunder with the proud.
>
> *(16:19)*

All these proverbs put in a nutshell an observation or com-ment about life in the raw, without stopping to bring all the individual comments into relationship with each other. This means that some of them seem to contradict each other. For instance, on the one hand,

> He who pursues righteousness and love
> finds life, prosperity and honour.
>
> *(21:21)*

But on the other hand,

> Better a little with righteousness
> than much gain with injustice.
>
> *(16:8)*

The second implicitly recognizes that the first is not always true. Or again, on the one hand,

> A bribe is a charm to the one who gives it;
> wherever he turns, he succeeds.
>
> *(17:8)*

But on the other,

> The prospect of the righteous is joy,
> but the hopes of the wicked come to nothing.
>
> *(10:28)*

The wise man, however, will not be floored by these apparent inconsistencies, because he knows how complex life is. He will not try to build a whole theory of life out of one observation.

And this brings us to the most basic point in the interpretation of Proverbs and the thing that opens up the book to us as Christians. What holds all these different sayings together is an underlying grasp of what wisdom really is. Chapters 1 – 9 are an extended essay on wisdom (in contrast to 'folly'), reaching a climax in chapters 8 and 9. Here we discover that wisdom is the Lord's, and that the Lord has exercised his wisdom in the creation of the world (8:22–31). Wisdom is, therefore, built into the fabric of things, and the wise person is the one who is able to live in harmony with the Creator and with his creation.

> The fear of the LORD is the beginning of wisdom,
> and knowledge of the Holy One is understanding.
>
> *(9:10)*

Because wisdom is built into the world, the person who 'fears' (loves, worships, obeys) God will begin to develop the profound perpectives on life opened up in the rest of the book. This is the way in which Proverbs joins the practical to the theological. And so we find that many of the proverbs reflect on life lived consciously in God's presence, or on what it means to fear him in practice. For instance:

> He who oppresses the poor shows contempt for their Maker,
> but whoever is kind to the needy honours God.
>
> *(14:31)*

> Do not say, 'I'll pay you back for this wrong!'
> Wait for the LORD, and he will deliver you.
>
> *(20:22)*

> The fear of the LORD leads to life:
> then one rests content, untouched by trouble.
>
> *(19:23)*

For us as Christians, 'wisdom' has taken on a new dimension.

The picture of wisdom in Proverbs 8:22–31 as a 'person' active in creation influenced the New Testament writers in their thinking about Jesus. Just as wisdom is God's agent in the process of creation in Proverbs, so Jesus is God's agent in creation in the New Testament (see especially Jn. 1:1–5; Col. 1:15–21; Heb. 1:1–4). And so Paul writes that Jesus 'has become for us wisdom from God' (1 Cor. 1:30), and speaks of 'Christ, in whom are hidden all the treasures of wisdom and knowledge' (Col. 2:3). So in Jesus we may begin to live in harmony with God and his world, and may begin to share the insights which the wise men of old developed as they, too, 'feared the Lord'. We can read Proverbs through Jesus, realizing that he shows us the 'wise' life at its fullest, and we can be stretched in our obedience to him as we think about the lifestyle Proverbs teaches.

Proverbs challenges us. When we read,

> Wise men store up knowledge,
> but the mouth of a fool invites ruin,
>
> *(10:14)*

we immediately want to know how we can avoid folly and learn wisdom. The answer of Proverbs is that 'the fear of the LORD is the beginning of wisdom' (9:10). But we have come to know the Lord in Christ, and so Proverbs points us to him.

The Song of Songs: the wise man in love

While Proverbs looks at life in general, the Song of Songs concentrates on human love and relationships, sex and marriage. It is a beautiful poem on these themes. The vital points to remember in handling it are these.

1. It is a dialogue

It is essential to use a translation, such as the NIV, which tells you who is speaking at each point. Sometimes it is the man ('lover') who speaks, sometimes the woman ('beloved') and sometimes a group of people ('friends'), who are called 'daughters of Jerusalem' in the poem itself.

2. It describes the course of a romance

The lover is Solomon himself. He refers in 6:8 to his other wives and concubines and, in 3:6–11, the girl describes his magnificent royal procession on their wedding day. She herself is a dark-skinned beauty (1:5) from Shulam in the north of the country (6:13). We read of their initial feelings about each other as she is brought to Solomon's court in Jerusalem (1:1 – 2:7); then of his proposal and their betrothal to each other and their longing for each other (2:8 – 3:5); of their wedding and the consummation of their love (3:6 – 5:1); then – so true to life! – we read of a breach in their relationship and of the restoration of their love. Their trust in each other even when apart, and the renewed quality of their love and commitment after their reconciliation, occupy the rest of the book (5:2 – 8:14).

It is a most beautiful and sensitive picture of married love. While there are some wonderful descriptions of each other's physical beauty, the poem focuses on the quality of their relationship, and the depth of their self-giving and commitment to each other. At the end, she wishes that Solomon had been her brother, so that they could have been together from childhood (8:1–4). Married couples should apply it to their own relationship and ask themselves how their love matches up to that of Solomon and his Shulammite. But it need not just apply to married people. I believe there is a further way in which it may be interpreted.

3. It is an allegory of God's love for his people, and *vice versa*

Within the Old Testament, marriage is frequently used as a picture of the relationship between Israel and the Lord, often involving unfaithfulness on Israel's part, and restoration. Hosea is a good example. As a prophet, he had to display the relationship between the Lord and Israel by marrying a prostitute, experiencing the pain of rejection and then showing the cost of forgiveness by buying her back (Ho. 1 – 3). Israel's rejection of God is often described as adultery, while the Lord is described as her faithful husband (*e.g.* Is. 54:5–7; Je. 2:1–3; 3:1–20; 31:32; Ezk. 16; 23).

This widespread use of marriage as a metaphor could be in mind in the Song of Songs. It is certainly open to us to interpret it in this way, especially when we turn to passages like Ephesians 5:22–32 and discover that marriage is also used as a picture of the relationship between Christ and his people, the church. Here, Paul specifically tells husbands and wives to pattern their love for each other on the self-giving love of Jesus, who 'left his Father' in order to be joined to his bride, the church.

But in fact the 'literal' and the 'allegorical' come together. Because Jesus is the 'wisdom' through whom the world was made, in all its beauty and complexity, we may deepen our knowledge of him through all our experiences of life and its relationships, and the experience of human love, self-giving and self-sacrifice stands out as special in this respect.

Applying the Songs of Songs today

There are a number of benefits to be gained from reading the Song of Songs today.

First, it can be read as a reminder to value one's husband or wife. It is easy to take him or her for granted. This song will challenge us about the depth of our commitment to and joy in each other.

Secondly, read it to help counter those negative views of marriage and sexuality that we can so easily absorb from society around. Marriage, for instance, is often portrayed as outmoded, restrictive and boring. Sexual relationships, on the other hand, are often shown in a debased way, as a matter of 'what I can get from' my partner. Solomon gives us a vision of something much better.

Thirdly, read the book as a reminder of the importance and fragility of close relationships. This book shows us that, whether we are married or single, a close relationship is developed and maintained only by devoting time to building it up and by taking care to protect it.

Finally, we can apply it to our relationship with Jesus. Do we cling to him as delightedly as this bride to her lover?

Ecclesiastes: the wise man in the world

Ecclesiastes is probably the most difficult of these books for us to handle today. It proclaims its message right at the start:

The words of the Teacher, son of David, king of Jerusalem:

'Meaningless! Meaningless!'
    says the Teacher.
'Utterly meaningless!
Everything is meaningless!'

(1:1–2)

This vigorous proclamation at the start accurately summarizes the message of the book: life is totally meaningless, according to this Teacher. He even calls wisdom meaningless in 1:12–18! The trouble is that this is exactly the opposite of what we tell people about Christ. In answer to the sense of meaninglessness felt by many today, we tell them that Christ can give meaning and purpose to their lives. It could be a little embarrassing if a potential convert opened the Bible at Ecclesiastes 1:1 and found that our own book confirms their initial feeling. What are we to do about this? Should we mentally remove it from our Bibles, or is there some way in which we can handle it as Christians?

One way forward is to suggest that the Teacher doesn't mean it. Maybe he is doing what the late Francis Schaeffer used to call 'pushing people to the logic of their own presuppositions'. In other words, perhaps he is describing what life is like when viewed solely from the perspective of this world, leaving God out of account – so as to show how necessary it is *not* to leave God out of account. This approach to Ecclesiastes has been adopted by many commentators in the past. But there is a problem with it; Ecclesiastes does not ignore God. It is true that he is never called 'the Lord', but he is none the less referred to no fewer than thirty-nine times.

Another way forward is to find contrasting viewpoints within the book itself. It is quite true that the Teacher sometimes seems to contradict himself. For instance, one moment he proclaims the meaninglessness of life, but the next he says:

> However many years a man may live,
>   let him enjoy them all . . .
> Be happy, young man, while you are young . . .
>   . . . banish anxiety from your heart . . .'
>
> *(11:8–10)*

Or else he complains about

> a righteous man perishing in his righteousness,
>   and a wicked man living long in his wickedness,
>
> *(7:15)*

only to do an about-turn in the next chapter:

> Because the wicked do not fear God, it will not go well with them, and their days will not lengthen like a shadow. *(8:13)*

Some have even felt that the book is a deliberately constructed debate between two viewpoints, one pessimistic and atheistic, and the other optimistic and religious – perhaps put together by someone who was compiling statements from different sources.

But again, this does not really fit the evidence. We saw that Proverbs, too, puts apparently contradictory statements side by side, knowing that both are true. There is no debate between them. And we can see that there is no debate in Ecclesiastes, either, when we meet verses like this:

Always be clothed in white, and always anoint your head with oil [a sign of rejoicing]. Enjoy life with your wife, whom you love, all the days of this meaningless life that God has given you under the sun – all your meaningless days. *(9:8–9)*

Here, God is charged with making life meaningless! Apparently the 'religious' outlook doesn't deny the meaninglessness of life; it supports it.

We begin to make progress when we ask what it is that makes life meaningless for the Teacher. The answer is easy: death. Death makes our existence meaningless because

- we cannot take anything with us, so our 'labour' in this life has no ultimate purpose (5:16);
- the same destiny comes to both the righteous and the wicked, so there is no ultimate point in trying to be righteous (9:2–3);
- you have to leave everything to others after your death and they may ruin your life's work: what then is the point of working? (2:18–23); and
- if human beings die like animals, who can claim that there is any difference between them (3:18–21)?

Death casts a ghastly shadow over everything:

'The fate of the fool will overtake me also.
  What then do I gain by being wise?'
I said in my heart,
  'This too is meaningless.'

(2:15)

The Teacher points to other 'evils' too, but this is the basic one. Death is not something that happens only to atheists and

183

the non-religious; it embraces all humankind, irrespective of their outlook. In fact, this is precisely what the Teacher complains about. Whether one is pious or not, death comes to all and makes all achievement meaningless. So this meaning-lessness is not one side of the contradiction, but underlies it. Why *do* the wicked live longer than the righteous, in a world in which they are not supposed to prosper? Because life is meaningless.

From a Christian point of view, we have to say that he is wrong. Our hope in Christ has transformed our outlook on death. The Teacher simply clung to his faith in God's ultimate judgment (3:15, 17), even though this contradicted the facts of life around him (3:16). We can now say much more about that final judgment and about life after death. Because of Jesus, we can see that it *does* matter whether we are righteous or wicked, wise or foolish.

On the other hand, he is not wholly wrong. In fact, he is not very wrong at all. Even as Christians, we still do not know why we are on this earth. We have no idea why evil is permitted, why judgment on the wicked is delayed, why God's children as well as other people have to suffer, or why God makes us labour at things which we know will fade and come to nothing in the end. We do not know why God created us, or what our ultimate purpose is, or why it was necessary for the world to fall and be redeemed. These are the great questions at the heart of our existence on the earth – and we do not know the answers to any of them. So for us, too, life is meaningless.

When I applied my mind to know wisdom and to observe man's labour on earth – his eyes not seeing sleep day or night – then I saw all that God has done. No-one can comprehend what goes on under the sun. Despite all his efforts to search it out, man cannot discover its meaning. Even if a wise man claims he knows, he cannot really comprehend it.   *(8:16–17)*

My colleague at London Bible College, Lish Eves, once told

me about a young American who got into a violent argument with a missionary, insisting that the missionary's faith was rubbish. Eventually this hot-tempered atheist went away with a copy of John's gospel to read, only to reappear a fortnight later with the news that he had become a Christian. When the missionary asked what part of John had touched him, he replied, 'John? It wasn't John at all; it was that Ecclesiastes! What a book! It's all so true!'

Yes, it is! The trouble is that we do not dare to be as honest as this good and wise man. But when we *are* as honest as he, the door is open to a deeper trust in God. We do not know, and yet we are in his hands (9:1). And we may also come to share his ringing verdict on it all:

> I know that there is nothing better for men than to be happy and do good while they live. That every man may eat and drink, and find satisfaction in all his toil – this is the gift of God.
> (3:12–13)

> Light is sweet,
> and it pleases the eyes to see the sun.
> However many years a man may live,
> let him enjoy them all.
>
> (11:7–8)

The vital thing, he tells us, is to enjoy life. This is not to escape from the 'meaninglessness' of our existence, but to face it honestly and to discover the peace that comes from facing it with God, and not against him. God has made life meaningless; he has created all these unanswerable questions by his ordering of the world. Nevertheless, to trust and fear him will mean that we can enjoy life in spite of its meaninglessness. Of course, the New Testament fills this out and shows us how, in Jesus, we may even know the miracle of joy in suffering (see, for instance, 1 Pet. 1:3–10).

Ecclesiastes brings us face to face with questions and facts that we would rather forget. It will keep us in touch with the deep questions being asked by many non-Christians today. The best way to read it is critically; this is certainly what the author would want. A book like this started its life in the meetings of the 'wise men', who doubtless argued over every point. Like them, we should attempt to disprove what the author says. Do his arguments hold water, as he seeks to prove the meaning-lessness of life? I believe that we shall in fact find it very difficult to overthrow his argument, except in that, because of Christ, we now know more about death and its destruction than he did. If we read Ecclesiastes critically like this, then we shall find our minds being stretched and our understanding of our own faith deepened.

Job: the wise man and his God

Job is one of the most 'contemporary' books of the Bible. In a good modern translation it is a deeply gripping read. We can easily identify with the story because it is about coping with an awful human tragedy. Like the Song of Songs, the book is a drama, with different speakers contributing to a passionate debate. The debate starts in heaven, between God and Satan (1:1–12), and then continues on earth between Job and his friends. Finally, God bursts into the debate with a marvellous revelation of himself which brings the book to a thrilling climax (chapters 38 – 42).

Job comes before Ecclesiastes in the Bible, but is the logical follow-on from it in two ways.

First, it tackles the contradiction between 'theology' and experience. The traditional theology of Job's day (derived from the teaching of books like Deuteronomy) said clearly that righteousness will lead to prosperity. But experience seemed to deny this; the righteous often suffer and the wicked often prosper. How should the God-fearing person, who struggles to keep God's laws, and has risked trusting God, explain this? Ecclesiastes, like Proverbs, simply holds both ideas alongside each other without explanation. Job faces the apparent contradiction and tries to understand it.

Secondly, it explores the personal relationship between humanity and God. This seems to lie at the heart of the message of Ecclesiastes, but is never really explored. The Teacher can 'enjoy' a meaningless life only because he is happy to accept it from God. How can he accept it like this? What kind of personal relationship with God does this mean? Job tackles this issue.

In Job we meet a man who faces in an acute form the meaninglessness of life on this earth. He has lost everything – property, job (he was self-employed), his children, his health and the support of his wife (1:13 – 2:10). There is no way he can enjoy what God has given him, because he has lost everything! But we, the readers, know why it has happened: God is proving to Satan that there are people who will love and trust him for his own sake, not for what they can get out of him. Satan argues that the relationship between God and Job rests simply on what each gets from the other; Job fears God only because of the blessings he has received from him (1:9–11). Is this true?

Underlying this test of Job's attitude to God, there is a deeper question about the nature of the relationship between God and humankind. Is it a 'contractual' relationship, based on the promise of 'blessings' in return for love and obedience? We instinctively react against the thought that it is. We somehow feel that we – and Job – should fear God for who he is, not for what he gives. But what is the alternative to a 'contractual' arrangement?

Job loses the 'blessings'. What is his reponse? If they were given contractually, then he should either curse God for breaking his side of the bargain (this is what Satan suggests he will do), or he should repent of the sins by which he must have broken his own side of the bargain; and this is what his three friends tell him he should do. They represent orthodox 'theology', which understood the relationship to be contractual. God blesses the righteous and punishes the wicked, so Job must be wicked! But Job refuses either to curse God or to repent. He insists that he has done nothing to deserve what God has done to him.

But in doing this – in denying that his relationship with God is contractual – *he makes life meaningless*. If God and humankind were tied together by the terms of a mutually beneficial contract ('You fear me, and I'll bless you'), then life would be meaningful and clear. But no such arrangement exists. Experience denies it. So Job sheds much light on Ecclesiastes and the reason for the Teacher's insistence on the meaninglessness of the world.

As the debate proceeds, Job reveals that what he longs for is not the restoration of what he has lost, but access to God. If only he could get to God and present his case, showing God how unjust this treatment is, he would be vindicated (13:18–24). Even so, he cannot believe that God is ignorant of the true facts:

> O earth, do not cover my blood;
> may my cry never be laid to rest!
> Even now my witness is in heaven;
> my advocate is on high.
>
> *(16:18–19)*

To cut a long story short, the book reaches its climax with God granting Job's longing to meet him. But Job does not speak when eventually he comes face to face with God. Instead, God displays the creation to Job in all its complexity and intricacy (chapters 38 – 39), and then in its mysteriousness and peculiarity (chapters 40 – 41). The hippopotamus ('behemoth') and the crocodile ('leviathan') were not just extraordinary animals, but also symbols of the powers of evil in the ancient world. We are as helpless before evil as we are before these mighty and peculiar animals; but God is equally in charge of both. Job receives no answers to his questions, and yet he is satisfied with this vision of a God who is the powerful and wise creator of a world which totally exceeds his power to comprehend. Life is still meaningless, but now Job knows God, and that is enough.

> My ears had heard of you,
>   but now my eyes have seen you.
> Therefore I despise myself
>   and repent in dust and ashes.
>
> *(42:5–6)*

The wise man has got to know his God. In fact, this is the message of the whole Bible. The Bible offers us not theoretical answers to our problems, but a living relationship with God himself, through Christ. In such a relationship of trust and love, it no longer matters that we do not know why the world is as it is. We are simply content to be part of it, knowing the one who has made it, and us, in infinite love, wisdom and power.

And to know God is the goal of all our Bible study, also. We cannot separate the Bible from the lives we lead. As we saw in chapters 2 and 3, God uses all our experiences of life in this world to shape our understanding of him. This is just what happened to Job. He started off believing that the righteous prosper and the wicked come to grief but, through his experience, he came to see that 'prosperity' is far more than just something outward and external. He found a prosperity of the spirit through his dreadful experience of loss and alienation.

In the same way, God will stretch and remake our knowledge of him through our lives, provided that, like Job, we keep coming back to his word and wrestling with it afresh in the light of our experience. Perhaps the greatest thing we need is that amazing honesty, which meant that Job did not hang back from saying exactly what he thought about God, while still refusing to curse him – and which meant that the Teacher could call life 'utterly meaningless' and yet still say,

> fear God and keep his commandments,
>   for this is the whole duty of man.
>
> *(Ec. 12:13)*

God has placed a guidebook into our hands to enable us to 'fear' him (shorthand for a whole intimate relationship of awe, trust, obedience and love). As we follow this guide, our lives will be rightly directed, however difficult the path. And part of the fun, as every hill-walker will tell you, is the satisfaction of successful map-reading and orientation. Using map and compass, an experienced walker can find the way through fog and bog, over featureless moors and through trackless forests, to safety and warmth on the other side. And that is exactly what the Bible will do for us, when rightly handled and applied to our lives.

The guides in the Crossway Bible Guide series have that glorious aim: to help us rightly handle God's Word, so that we may find the path and stay on it until we arrive home safely with our heavenly Father. The Bible with *pleasure*: that's our purpose. And not just the pleasure of studying it, on our own or in a group. Even more than that: it's the pleasure of the marathon runner at 23 miles, who knows he has enough stamina to stay ahead and complete the race; the pleasure of the student in the exam room, who looks at the questions and knows that she can answer them really well; the pleasure of the parents at their son's wedding, as they look at him and say, 'Yes, we did a pretty good job; it was tough but worth it. He'll be all right!' It's the pleasure of those who know that they have built their lives on the Rock, so that whatever storms come, they will be secure. That's the pleasure the Bible gives to those who treasure it as the guide to the Way we travel to the Heavenly City.